PÂTÉS, TERRINES AND POTTED MEATS

Cookery adviser: Elizabeth David

Pâtés, Terrines and Potted Meats

Simone Sekers

B. T. BATSFORD LTD, LONDON

Drawings by Judith Hamp

First published 1978
Copyright Simone Sekers 1978
ISBN 0 7134 0679 8

Set in VIP Palatino by Trident Graphics Ltd, Reigate, Surrey
Printed by The Anchor Press Ltd, Tiptree, Essex
for the publishers B. T. Batsford Ltd,
4 Fitzhardinge Street, London W1H 0AH

Contents

Acknowledgements

I would like to thank the following people for their help in compiling this book: Janet Clarke and her wonderful stock of historic cookery books; David Collins – for his recipe on page 32; Bernard Sandall, Deputy Editor of the Stoke-on-Trent *Evening Sentinel*, for his permission to quote the passage on page 8; and my family and friends who patiently and good-humouredly ate their way through so many of the recipes in this book.

For further reading on the subject covered by this book, I recommend, very highly, the following:

Elizabeth David *English Potted Meats and Fish Pastes*, Elizabeth David, 1968.
Jane Grigson *Charcuterie and French Pork Cookery*, Michael Joseph, 1967 and Penguin Books; *Good Things*, Michael Joseph, 1971 and Penguin Books; *English Food*, Macmillan, 1974.
Dorothy Hartley *Food in England*, Macdonald, 1954
Sheila Hutchins *English Recipes*, Methuen, 1967.

as well as all the old cookery books I have quoted and mentioned throughout.

Introduction

Traditions

I hope to achieve, in this book, the marriage of two great culinary traditions – those of French and English *charcuterie*. How often one returns from a holiday in France with the memories of delicious pâtés eaten beside poplar-fringed canals, or rustic terrines appearing as part of a simple meal in a modest *routier*; the memories are stored away and we accept with resignation the only charcuterie that this country has to offer – pork pies with sinister grey eggs entombed inside, or sausages oozing cereal, gristle and artificial colouring.

But what happened to our traditional raised pies and potted meats? At what point did they retire from our kitchens and tables? Perhaps one clue to the mystery lies in the deep-freeze. Pâtés, terrines, raised pies, potted meats and pastes were all variations on methods of preserving. With improved means of feeding cattle and better trade organisation during the eighteenth century, it became easier to obtain meat during the winter and preserving became less long-term, though still necessary in order to provide a household with a constant supply. Potted meats began to replace the more basic methods of salting or smoking, although these still had their place. Both the development of commercial canning between the two World Wars, and the rise of the domestic freezer, with its amiable ability to store meat without having to change its state first, caused these methods, all requiring time and trouble, to disappear. In France, where people care more deeply about the quality of their food this change is less noticeable. The French housewife can still buy good products from her local *charcutier* almost every day of the week and would consider herself and her family deprived of one of the basic ingredients of life if she could not.

The deep-freeze is not the only culprit in the sad story of the fall of English cooked meats. Another can be found in the evolution of industrial life, which caused families to move from the country to the towns and cities, where they were no longer able to keep the pig which had hitherto kept them stocked with an almost year-long supply of meat. The lack of this precious supply gave rise to, first the necessity, and then the popularity, of less healthy food including tinned meat and fish and commercial meat and fish pastes. It would seem, however, that in the North of England (and I would draw a line running just south of Birmingham here) men moving into the huge conurbations that grew up during the Industrial Revolution could not bear to leave behind the heavy rustic dishes that their own pigs had once provided. There still exists a strong tradition of pork cookery in these northern towns; in the Black Country, pubs serve 'scratchings' instead of crisps with their beer – squares of pork crackling, exactly the same as the *rillons* served to us with such a flourish in a smart Lyonnais restaurant. And only the other day I found this paragraph in our local evening paper:

> 'PIG'S EAR. The increasing cost of food could herald the return of dishes which lost their appeal as the affluent society got to grips with steak and scampi. For, as any pensioner knows, the Magnificent Seven are not Yul Brynner and his mates – but the traditional Potteries fare of tripe, brawn, brains, udder, trotters, giblets and black pudding. There is one amusing story about an irate gentleman who took a slice of brawn back to a Hanley shop, complaining that it contained a piece of pig's ear, and was duly given a fresh quarter and an apology. It just goes to show that there are times when an Englishman very definitely draws the line, when good taste is threatened, for we are assured by a connoisseur that a pig's snout and ears should be omitted when the dish is prepared.'
> (Stoke-on-Trent *Evening Sentinel*)

There is a firm of pork butchers in Kendal, Cumbria, whose windows rival those of any French *charcuterie*, and whose 'bridge pies' cause one expatriate, exiled in London, to wax lyrical in their praise. After holidays in the Lake District, I bring yards of pure pork Cumberland sausage down to friends living in less privileged parts of the country. Here, in Stoke-on-Trent, a visit to any of the twice- and sometimes thrice-weekly covered markets held in each of the six Pottery towns reveals rows of pork stalls with glistening 'head cheeses', or brawns, galantines, savoury ducks (faggots), pots of delicious dripping with a layer of gravy at the bottom, black puddings, white puddings, rashers of pork fat, and of home-cured bacon, ropes of sausages and swags of tripe. Faced with this bounty, it is sad to realise that it is often the elderly who shop at these stalls – the younger women seem to prefer the sausages and pork pies to be bought in bulk from the morgue-like freezer centre down the road.

Having established, therefore, that the rudiments of our own tradition still exist, I would like to elaborate on the English themes with the help of some French recipes. The basic ingredients are all here, and as continental cookery in general has aroused much interest, the spices and herbs necessary are available in almost every supermarket. Nearly all the recipes require pork, and often the cheapest cuts are the best to use.

I wish I had room in this book to cover the whole range of pork and cooked meat products on both sides of the Channel. I am limiting myself, with difficulty, to pâtés, terrines, galantines, raised pies, potted meats and pastes, with examples from both countries, where possible, in each chapter.

Origins and Parallels

The origins of the words *pâté* and *terrine* are fairly well-defined; both words describing the container in which the ingredients were originally cooked – the pâté within a crust of pastry and the terrine baked in a pottery dish. So at once we can draw parallels between the French dishes and those of our own country, the *pâté* with the raised pie and the *terrine* with potted meat.

Descriptions of meat baked in a pastry-case, or 'coffin', appear in medieval cookery books and a recipe for 'Steake Pye' dated 1658 (page 60) still uses this lugubrious name to describe the crust. English raised pies reached their zenith with the tremendous Yorkshire pies of the eighteenth century – these were constructed by filling various boned poultry and game birds with forcemeat and packing them into a hot-water-paste crust. Any spare corners were packed with more forcemeat and the finished product was solid enough to be exported to various parts of the country. I have quoted Mrs Raffald's famous recipe for a 'Yorkshire Goose-Pie' in the chapter on raised pies – partly because it is a classic piece of cookery writing and partly as an inspiration to try at least an approximation of it for a special occasion.

By the nineteenth century, however, pies began to go out of fashion; cookery books gave recipes for alternatives – 'puptons', 'pulpatoons' and 'tureens'. Firms like Spode and Wedgwood began to make elegant lidded tureens, often decorated to imitate the elaborate pie-crusts once so popular (although during his period as cook to Charles II, Patrick Lamb describes a 'Terryné-Dish' made in silver which was used at Court. He also gives a complicated recipe for a 'Hampton Court Pupton', though he does not specify that the silver tureen was used to cook it in). There is an idea that the development of 'pie-crust pottery' coincided with the scarcity and resulting high prices of flour at the end of the Napoleonic Wars. The Corn Laws of 1815, followed by a sequence of poor harvests, caused a dearth of grain all over the country, and these events could possibly provide a reason for the use of earthenware instead of pastry to enclose baked meat. Raised pies retired to more rustic tables and the tureens emerged in elegant society. A lining of forcemeat within the tureen itself enclosed anything from homely pigeons to imaginative mixtures of oysters, sweetbreads, cockscombs, sometimes asparagus and often mushrooms. These could be eaten hot (as in the case of puptons), or cold, which was more often the case with tureens. I have included recipes for both dishes (pages 43, 46) as they make good use of small amounts of ingredients and are therefore surprisingly economical as well as good. Alexis Soyer, in 1850, in *The Modern Housewife* describes how he 'bought the other day a common earthen tureen for which I gave ninepence'; he then gives a recipe for lining it with forcemeat, adding a boned grouse and seasoning, sealing it and baking it for three hours: 'when I opened it about a week afterward it was most delicious'. This reads so like a recipe for a French 'Terrine de Gibier' that the resemblances between English tureens and French *terrines* are obvious. Mrs Harriet de Salis, writing *Sweets and Supper Dishes à la Mode* nearly 50 years after Soyer, in 1898, states that 'china dishes are now so generally used and so much prettier than the pastry cases, that I shall here only give a recipe for filling the china dishes'. Fashions in food progressed very slowly, and raised pies still featured on menus, though more generally in gentlemen's clubs, at shooting picnics and in country inns – ladies' appetites presumably becoming smaller as corsets became ever more restricting.

Galantines, like puptons and tureens, also originated in the raised pie. Boned birds, stuffed with forcemeat, often formed the filling of these pies as I have already described, and in his entry on galantines in *The Book of the Table*, Kettner warns that terrines sold in shops in London as 'Yorkshire pies' were in fact 'galantines in pots'. It is still a popular dish both in this country and in France – not surprisingly, as a small chicken, stuffed with a good mixture of pork and surrounded by its own jelly, will feed 9–10 people, and is a good deal easier and cheaper to make than its impressive appearance would indicate. The origin of the name has been much discussed, but even Kettner comes to no clear conclusion. Of the various theories, one is that it comes from 'galingale', a spice of the ginger family used in flavouring the earliest recipes for similar dishes, and another that 'gelatine' has something to do with the derivation, as jelly forms an important part of the dish. The most interesting and plausible explanation is that it stems from an eighteenth-century French *charcutier*'s term for dressing a pig in a particular manner. Certainly by the beginning of the nineteenth century the word was widely used in France to describe the dish we now know as a galantine.

Puptons, tureens and galantines were frivolous dishes compared with the more practical and stolid potted meats, whose sole purpose was to preserve (although Esther Copley, in 1834, describes the idea of potting to 'afford animal food to those who have not the means of chewing it', undoubtedly an important consideration before the days of modern dentistry).

When cattle, or the family pigs, were killed in the autumn, having been fattened to this end all summer, almost all of the animal that was not already 'owed' to various tradesmen in payment of debts run up during hard times, had to be made to see the family through the winter. The offal was eaten immediately, although in France sausages were made from it which were also cured and helped to enliven the monotony of the winter diet. A fascinating description of the life of the cottager's pig, its execution and the preservation of its meat is given in one of the opening chapters of Flora Thompson's *Lark Rise to Candleford*, while William Cobbett devotes a large part of his *Cottage Economy* to this vital area of housekeeping; in the first book of John Moore's 'Brensham Trilogy', mention is made of the rosemary bush to be found growing in every cottage garden, to flavour the lard from the pig – spread on toast or bread it must have been better than the butter that few of the cottagers could afford in any case.

The simplest methods, and the most ancient, were used to cure this vital supply of meat – it was either salted in dry salt, or in a brine, or it was smoked. These processes produced strong flavoured meat, to which poorer people made no objection. On farms and in large houses, however, where a slightly more regular supply of meat was available, it could be preserved in more refined and less vigorous ways, using expensive ingredients such as quantities of butter, and spices. The meat, or fish, to be preserved was rubbed with salt and spices and left for a day or two, before being covered with plenty of fat – lard or butter – and a little liquid, and cooked, in a covered pot, in a slow oven. When done, it was removed and drained thoroughly of its juices, before being finely chopped, re-spiced and sealed with clarified fat. Until the seal was broken on a jar of potted meat, it could be stored safely for several weeks. Dorothy Hartley, in *Food in England*, has an interesting chapter on the various ways of salting, drying and preserving, with a fascinating recipe for potting poultry whole for export, and a theory that we owe our recipes for pressed and potted meats to the early days of sailing ships. Judging by the many descriptions of unattractive shipboard food in the seventeenth, eighteenth and nineteenth centuries, salt beef and pork, becoming harder and drier as the voyage progressed, was probably the most common food for sailors.

The French equivalents of English potted meats are the famous *confits*, usually of goose, pork or duck. These are usually served hot, because of their rich fatty texture; *confit d'oie* is an essential ingredient of *cassoulet*, that monumental stew of haricot beans, sausages and joints of meat which originated in Toulouse. Their English counterparts most often appeared on the cold table.

The distinction between potted meats and meat pastes is sometimes blurred, but pastes were always made from left-overs of game, meat, poultry, fish and cheese, pounded with butter and spices and sealed in the same way, with clarified butter. These were used in sandwiches and as relishes for breakfast or supper. Parson Woodforde must have eaten tongue paste when he wrote in his diary for 7 October 1794 'We had for breakfast, Chocolate, green and brown Tea, hot Rolls, dried Toast, Bread and Butter, Honey, Tongue and ham grated very small.' Richard Bradley's recipe, in his delightful book *The Country Housewife*, published in 1753, 'To pot a cold Tongue, Beef or Venison', must have been very like that eaten by Parson Woodforde: 'Cut it small, beat it well in a Marble Mortar, with melted Butter and two Anchovies, till the Meat is mellow and fine; then put it down close in your Pots, and cover it with clarified Butter.' The lavish breakfasts eaten by George Borrow in the 1850s on his trip through 'Wild Wales' included potted trout, hare, and shrimps, and of these, the 'pot of hare' was probably hare paste, perhaps made from the remains of a jugged hare.

The only versions of these pastes that occur in French cookery are the pork *rillettes*, which are a speciality of the Touraine. They are a great standby in our house and I give a recipe for them on page 71.

The English fondness for large breakfasts and high teas goes a long way to explain the existence of so many potted delicacies. French *saucissons* do not serve the same purpose, being served hot as a main course, or cold and sliced as part of an *hors d'oeuvre*. I have not given them a chapter in this book as their manufacture calls for processes, ingredients and equipment not needed by other recipes here. For anyone wanting to try them, Jane Grigson's book *Charcuterie and French Pork Cookery* covers the subject both thoroughly and inspiringly.

Conclusions and Revivals

When trying to divide the recipes in this book into separate chapters, the only difficulty I found, apart from the potted meats and pastes, as I explained earlier, was drawing a line between pâtés and terrines. Despite the origins of the two names, destinctions between the two dishes have become vague – here in England as well as in France. My own definition is the one I have used, it is a personal view and therefore likely to be argued with; pâtés I class as a more elegant and refined version of the terrine, which I think of as a simpler, more rustic dish. If you are looking for a sophisticated first course for a dinner party look in the pâté chapter, and in the chapter on terrines for a recipe suitable for a picnic lunch or a buffet supper.

The generous habit of keeping these dishes available in the still-room for friends and travellers who arrived with little or no notice, has been superseded by the more grudging one of keeping food in the freezer. Freezers need forethought and forewarning to be used to their best advantage; potted meats and terrines carefully stored in a cold larder, or refrigerator, are always ready to eat – with the accompaniment of good bread, salad and a glass of wine they can make a memorable meal, prepared in minutes. Use the freezer for storing the raw ingredients, but keep the finished product out of it; properly prepared it will keep for weeks and taste the better for it – *'Meat in the house* is a great source of *harmony'* – how right Cobbett was.

Simone Sekers, 1978

PART ONE

Herbs and Spices

Wherever possible, grow your own herbs and buy your spices loose from chemists. Avoid falling for powdered spices and herbs in pretty glass jars as they often have little flavour left and you are in fact paying for the jar – if you can find black tin spice boxes or those lovely wooden spice 'towers' in an antique shop, go for those as they are the best way of storing spices, away from air *and* light.

Allspice *(Pimenta officinalis)*
The whole berries are often available from Boots, and as with ordinary pepper it is better to crush or grind the berries as they are needed (I have a separate pepper grinder for allspice), than to buy it in powdered form. It can be used in place of *quatre-épices* in most pâté recipes.

Bay leaves *(Laurus nobilis)*
These are so indispensable in the kitchen that it is well worth growing this very beautiful tree (in a tub, so that it can be brought in from frost in the winter). Dried bay leaves quickly lose their flavour, so buy them in small quantities. They are useful for their decorative qualities in terrines, as well as for their uniquely aromatic taste.

Cayenne pepper *(Capsicum frutescens)*
This pungent member of the pepper family is best used for the meat, fish and cheese pastes. Buy it in powdered form, in small quantities, from chemists, and keep in an air and light-tight container.

Celery *(Apium graveoleus dulce)*
Chopped celery leaves, used fresh in season in the blander pâtés and in chicken galantine, give a good 'green' flavour, when other fresh herbs are not available. It is also invaluable for flavouring stocks and aspics.

Chervil *(Anthriscus cerefolium)*
A hardy annual looking like delicate parsley, it will seed itself readily each year. It tastes a little like tarragon – a mild aniseed flavour, particularly good with chicken.

Cinnamon *(Cinnamomum zeylanicum)*
For the recipes in this book it is most useful in its best-known, powdered, form; it is also one of the ingredients of *quatre-épices.* It too should be bought in small quantities and stored away from light and air. Whole cinnamon sticks, available from chemists, have more flavour and can be used in this form in game aspic.

Cloves *(Eugenia aromatica)*
Powdered cloves also form part of *quatre-épices*, and small amounts are good in the game recipes. An onion stuck with cloves is an important part of the seasoning for stocks and jellies.

Coriander *(Coriandrum satinum)*
This lovely spice should always be used freshly crushed as its elusive orangey scent quickly disappears in its powdered form. Delicious in pork pies and chicken liver paste.

Garlic *(Allium sativum)*
If you live in a warm area, this can easily be grown in the garden; in colder
areas the bulbs do not grow very large, nor do they have much flavour.
Imported garlic is available in many small-town greengrocers now and
provided it feels nice and solid, it is worth buying, rather than struggling to
produce your own. Garlic powders have very little merit – you often find
yourself adding too much salt with them, and as the garlic clove itself is so
convenient and well packaged, I cannot see the point of buying the *ersatz*
variety. *Chopped* garlic has a milder and less acrid flavour than *crushed* garlic.
A small wire or wicker basket, which can be hung on a hook near the
cooker, is a very good way of storing garlic, as this is one of the flavourings
that does appreciate the free flow of air around it.

Ginger *(Zingiber officinale)*
Again, used in small quantities in the recipes in this book, and in
quatre-épices. Dried ginger root, which is preferable to the powder and is
available from chemists, is easily grated on a nutmeg grater.

Juniper *(Juniperus communis)*
These berries, like large black peppercorns, are invaluable for flavouring
pâtés and many other pork dishes. It is a good idea to buy a large amount
when you see them, as they keep well and are not always easy to find; a
cocoa-tin is an ideal container. Crush them lightly before using.

Mace *(myristica fragrans)*
The outer husk of the nutmeg, its flavour is like that of nutmeg and
cinnamon mixed. The lovely golden-brown filigree 'blades' of mace are
difficult to find now, and it is most widely available in powder form.

Marjoram *(Marjorana hortensis)*
An annual easily grown in sheltered gardens. Good in galantines and pork
pies.

Mixed spices
  – see *Quatre-épices*

Nutmeg *(Myristica fragrans)*
Much used in charcuterie products and best bought whole and grated

freshly when needed. Whole nutmegs are sold by most chemists and a nutmeg grater with a compartment at the back to hold the nutmeg is a useful, cheap and decorative gadget.

Parsley *(Petroselinum crispum)*
This is essential in the kitchen. It is easily grown, but if bought fresh can be kept in a polythene box in the fridge. Dried parsley is not worth buying.

Pepper *(Piper nigrum)*
Black and white peppercorns are easily obtainable from chemists; use the black pepper for fragrance and the white for strength, or mix the two together, as they do in France. Invest in a good peppermill or two and always use pepper freshly ground, both in the kitchen and at the table. Soft green peppercorns are now more widely available in this country, particularly from specialist grocers like Jacksons, Harrods and Fortnums, but are not as expensive as this would imply. They come in small jars or tins of brine and can be kept in the fridge. Drained of the brine and lightly crushed, they give a unique flavour to many pâtés and terrines, especially duck and pheasant.

Pistachio *(Pistacia vera)*
The 'green' flavour of these nuts, and their texture, gives them a special place in the more sophisticated pâtés and galantines. They can be used as a cheaper alternative to truffles.

Quatre-épices
A blend of spices used in French charcuterie, and very useful to keep, ready-mixed, in small quantities, for English recipes as well. Use the spices in their powdered form.

> *Blend I*   1 teasp. each ground cloves, cinnamon and nutmeg to 7 teasps black pepper or 6 teasps white pepper.
> *Blend II*   2 ozs white pepper; 2 teasps ground cloves; ½ oz. ground ginger; ½ oz. ground nutmeg.

Sage *(Salvia officinalis)*
Used sparingly in French charcuterie, though often over-generously in English cooked meats. It is a pretty, easily grown shrub, in many varieties, including Red Sage and a variegated type which is very decorative.

Salt
I keep my expensive sea-salt for the table and use ordinary cooking-salt (block salt when I can get it) in the kitchen.

Saltpetre *(Potassium nitrate)*
An ingredient used in salting meat, helping to preserve the colour of the meat which would otherwise go an unappetising grey. It is used in very small quantities as it hardens the meat (sugar is used to counteract this), and has no other preservative qualities. Buy it from chemists, an ounce or two at a time as it absorbs moisture. Store it in a polythene bag in a screw-top jar in a dry place.

Spiced salt *(Sel-épicé)*
Used like *quatre-épices* in French charcuterie, it is made in larger quantities and is not as subtle.

> Blend 2 lbs block or sea salt; 8 ozs ground white pepper; 7 ozs powdered mixed spice.

Tarragon *(Artemisia dracunculus)*
A pretty feathery plant which is best grown indoors unless your garden is warm and sheltered. Make quite sure you buy the true French variety, the type known as 'Russian' is much hardier but has little flavour. If you use dried tarragon, go carefully as it is strong and can give a musty flavour.

Thyme *(Thymus vulgaris)*
A great winter standby, especially for rabbit pies and terrines. Easily grown, with many varieties including a variegated one. Lemon thyme is good with chicken.

Truffles
A great luxury but worth it to make a pâté for a celebration. Truffle-peelings are also available and are marginally cheaper; both are sold in minute as well as larger amounts and a tin or two can be the best souvenir of a French holiday.

Equipment

I do not suppose that you will need to buy many of the items on the following list – they are all things that most of us have in our kitchens in any case. It is a good idea to keep your eyes open in junk shops for dishes and jars and drainers; the faded Victorian colours and designs suit pies and terrines much better than bright modern counterparts. Pearsons of Chesterfield have done an enormous amount to circulate their delightful traditional stoneware cooking pots throughout the country, at modest prices. The most important single item of equipment, however, is bound to be:

The mincer

Cookery books have a habit of talking about your helpful butcher mincing ingredients for you. Times have changed, as fewer and fewer butchers seem to have the time, or inclination, for this sort of service. With your own mincer you can vary the textures of your pies and pâtés, which is important; even the most complicated recipe can be monotonous if the consistency of the forecemeat is always the same.

There is an excellent mincer attachment for the Kenwood Chef, with three different screens, and a sausage-making gadget if you want to turn your forecemeat into sausages. Purists prefer to chop the meat for pâtés, as this reserves the juices – mincing tends to squeeze them out. The only machine that will do this for you automatically is the Magimix, but at nearly £80 it is a major purchase unless you are looking for your first electric mixer. Spong are still doing good hand-operated mincers which have advantages over the electric ones – cheapness, compactness, reliability and quietness – but a sizeable disadvantage, it can be very hard work mincing a large amount of meat.

Containers

What you choose to cook your terrines and pâtés in will largely be determined by whether or not you are going to store them in their containers. A bread tin, lined with foil, is perfectly adequate for the grandest pâté if you are then going to serve it on an appropriate dish – the foil lining can be wrapped round the pâté and the whole kept until needed. Otherwise, a good, plain stoneware terrine, preferably, but not essentially, with its own lid, is better than an earthenware one. Earthenware has a relatively short oven-life – the glaze begins to crack, and into these cracks seep fats and juices which go stale, this staleness then running subsequent dishes. My favourite containers are those in flame-coloured vitrified ironware by Le Creuset, their cost is more than justified by their long life and comfortingly professional look. It is worth noting that when cooking pâtés in metal containers, about 15 minutes should be knocked off the cooking time. Ovenproof porcelain is also good, and surprisingly strong.

The size of the container used is also important, most significantly where too large a container is used for too small a quantity of the mixture, which will lead to overcooking. It is the depth of the mixture in its cooking container which counts in reckoning cooking time, rather than its weight. As the meat in this type of dish shrinks quite a bit in the cooking it is essential that intially the container be packed quite full to the brim and slightly domed in the centre. If not the cooked dish could end up looking rather sad and lost in its container as well as being overcooked.

To determine the container you need, allow approximately 1 pint capacity for every 1½ lb mixture. So a 1¼ pint bowl will hold about 2 lb mixture and a 2½ pint bowl will hold at least 3½ lb mixture and a 2½ pint bowl will hold at least 3½ lb. An extra 4–6 oz can usually be fitted in by packing the mixture more solidly.

For galantines, which need a mould, the simplest shape possible is the one to aim for. Large mixing bowls or salad bowls, or oval earthenware casseroles, will do very well.

Potted meats need the same containers as pâtés and terrines for the initial cooking but for the secondary, storage, stage, simple straight-sided pottery jars, or Kilner jars, look best. For meat pastes, white china ointment jars, or those old-fashioned Keiller marmalade jars are ideal. When you find them on china stalls, check that the glaze inside the pot is sound, with no crazing.

Pies can be raised by hand, or round a well-floured glass jar, but the proper way to do it is round a wooden pie-mould. These are often found in junk-shops and are somewhat club-shaped. If your family shows appreciation of your pies, it is worth asking them to contribute towards a proper hinged pie-mould. Beautifully made of pressed tin, with brass pins to hold the sides together, and a removable base, they make the production of perfect, elaborate and beautiful pies practically foolproof. They are expensive, but well worth the cost.

Drainers

When making potted meats it is essential to drain off all the gravy and juices, so that they can be stored safely over long periods. For this purpose, china drainers, or those to be found inside fish and ham kettles, are better than cake racks or sieves as they are easier to clean. Look for these, too, on junk stalls; usually oval, with a large hole in the middle and smaller ones radiating out from the centre, in plain white or transfer-printed china, they were originally made to fit into large platters so that vegetables, especially asparagus, could be served 'dry', instead of sitting in pools of water in vegetable dishes.

Knives

Really sharp knives are as important as a mincer. Choose knives made of carbon steel, they can be made far sharper than stainless steel ones, and to keep them sharp, store them in a wooden or magnetic knife rack, where they are always within reach. Some of my favourite knives have been found in 5p baskets of old cutlery – a straight-bladed knife, long and flexible, for carving ham, a short knife with an almost triangular blade from long years of sharpening which is perfect for boning poultry. Knives bought one by one as you find you need them are often more useful than extravagently presented sets.

Other cutting gadgets

MEZZALUNA – this is a semicircular blade, sometimes with one handle in the middle, sometimes with one at each end, and often with its own wooden cutting dish, and it has a million uses. It is particularly useful for chopping several different ingredients at once – herbs, juniper berries, lemon peel and garlic, for instance, for a rabbit terrine. It is inexpensive and very easy to clean.

MOULI-PARSMINT – one of the useful Mouli range; very good for small amounts of herbs.

ZYLISS AUTO-CHOP – this consists of a sharp zig-zag of stainless steel, enclosed in a plastic dome; a flat plastic knob on a spring emerges like a stalk from the top of the dome. To use it, you simply put your meat, vegetables, nuts, herbs or whatever on a board, place the dome over the top and bang the handle up and down with the palm of your hand. In seconds the food is finely and evenly chopped. It is particularly good for making *rillettes*, giving them the right grainy texture.

Chopping-board
I like good, thick heavy boards without joins, perfectly flat and of a reasonable size. Buy the best you can afford as they last for years. I do not like decorated melamine; it is too light, and scars easily, quickly looking sordid.

An old baking-tin
Or something similar, for standing your terrines in hot water in the oven. A proper *bain-marie* is expensive and not really necessary.

Mixing-bowls
Try to have several, at least two really large ones, three or four medium sized ones, and the same number of small ones (pudding-basins will do). If you have a market near you, it will probably have a 'seconds' stall where you can buy bowls more cheaply than in an ironmonger's.

Large saucepan
A really large one is essential for cooking galantines. If you can lay your hands on a ham or fish kettle, complete with drainer to enable you to lower your bird gently into the simmering stock, so much the better.

Sieves
One large and one small, so that they can be lined with muslin and used when clarifying stock and butter.

Kitchen haberdashery and stationery
These are all the small bits and pieces that you are liable to need for a lot of the recipes in this book, and for cooking in general: foil, waxed paper, polythene bags in assorted sizes, string and/or cotton tape, linen button-thread and a large-eyed, blunt tapestry needle for sewing up poultry, lots of muslin for clarifying, wrapping galantines, and tying up whole spices before adding them to a brine or stock. Old muslin nappies and handkerchiefs, well-boiled first of course, do very well for this sort of work.

Weights, Measures and Temperatures

Despite the advance of metrication, I think it will be some time before we use it in the privacy of our kitchens. Because I think it confusing to have metric and English measures given side by side in recipes (a practice which ruined an otherwise excellent cookery book published recently), I am giving this table of comparative weights, measures and oven temperatures at the beginning, to refer to when necessary.

Solid measures

Metric	English (approx.)
1 kilo (1000 grammes)	2 lb 3 oz
500 gr	1 lb 1½ oz
250 gr	9 oz
125 gr	4¼ oz
100 gr	3½ oz

Liquid measures

Metric	English
1 litre	1¾ pints (35 fl oz)
½ litre	just over ¾ pint (17½ fl oz)
¼ litre	just under ½ pint (8¾ fl oz)
1 decilitre	about 3 fl oz
1 centilitre	about 1 dessertspoon

Gas and electric oven temperatures

°F	°C		Gas
250°F	120°C	Very slow	½
275°F	140°C	Slow	1
300°F	150°C		2
325°F	160°C	Warm	3
350°F	180°C	Moderate	4
375°F	190°C	Fairly hot	5
400°F	200°C	Hot	6
425°F	220°C		7
450°F	230°C	Very hot	8
475°F	240°C		9
500°F	250°C		10

Golden Rules

None of these rules need be followed to the letter – pâté-making is extraordinarily easy, if sometimes lengthy – but they will all contribute to the success of your efforts.

Flavour

1) Tasting: many people worry, not unreasonably, about tasting a mass of raw meat for seasoning. While that mass is waiting to be cooked (see below), fry a small piece and let it get quite cold. It is important to allow it time to cool, as that is how you will be eating it and seasonings need to be more pronounced in cold food. Taste this cooked piece and adjust the herbs, salt, spices or alcohol accordingly.

2) Waiting: the raw mixture will improve with waiting while you test for seasoning; in some recipes it is a good idea to leave the meats overnight to give the flavours a chance to blend. In any case, let them stand for about 2 hours before cooking.

3) Maturing: after cooking, leave the terrine for at least two days before eating. In the winter, a week is about right, and it need not be kept in the fridge if you have a cool larder.

4) Room Temperature: if you have been keeping your pâté or paste in the fridge, or if your larder is very cold, bring it into room temperature for an hour or two before serving – otherwise your carefully blended flavours will be lost.

Textures

Try to vary the texture in pâtés and terrines; there are many ways of doing this – by altering the screens on the mincer; by cutting pork fat into cubes and mixing these with the meat; by layering finely minced forcemeat with whole pieces of game.

You will find all pâtés and terrines easier to cut, or turn out, if you put a gentle weight on top of them as they cool. I usually do this by covering the top of the dish with foil and then putting two tins (on their sides) on top. Leave overnight and then remove the tins.

Decoration

If you intend to turn your pâté out, decorate the bottom of the terrine before piling in the forcemeat. I usually use combinations – of not more than two at a time – of bay leaves, juniper berries, green peppercorns, cranberries (for game) and sprigs of fresh rosemary, depending on what I have used to season the pâté. If you are leaving the pâté in its dish, decorate the top; very often the lattice of pork fat strips used for basting is the nicest and simplest ornament. For galantines you can be a little more elaborate, cutting shapes from the surrounding jelly, or using lemon slices, tarragon leaves, chervil, or other fresh herbs. I avoid the piped-mayonnaise style.

Raised pies present no problem – you can express yourself with exuberance in the pastry itself. Remember to glaze it with yolk of egg. Potted meats and pastes, with their crusts of white lard or yellow butter contrasting with the pale pink of the contents, need only a sprig of parsley to make them look delicious. Surround a pot of fish paste with lemon wedges.

Freezing
Simply – don't. If you have to keep the pâté or terrine longer than intended, pour a layer of lard to a depth of ¼" over the top, wrap the whole thing, dish and all, in foil and store in the refrigerator. Certainly never freeze anything which is in aspic.

PART TWO

Pâtés

Pâtés are the aristocrats of charcuterie – they call for the subtlest seasoning, the most expensive ingredients, and sometimes the greatest expenditure of time as well. They are not difficult however, and are wonderful dishes for celebrations; they do deserve good wines to drink with them. There are no traditional English recipes which correspond to the French ones, but there are modern English equivalents and generally I have given these English names.

Pâté de Chartres (for 6–8)

1¼ lb fat belly pork, rind removed
½ lb lean veal
¼ lb chicken livers
2 large egg yolks
4 oz double cream
1 lb puff pastry (frozen will do)
¾ pint aspic (page 82)
¾ oz *quatre-épices*
1 small glass brandy
1 small glass port or madeira
Salt and freshly ground pepper

¼ lb tongue
¼ lb ham
¼ lb lean veal
¼ lb pork fat
} cut into strips and put to marinate in a mixture of 2 tblsps brandy and 6 crushed juniper berries

Mince the first three items finely, putting them twice through the finest screen. Beat in the egg yolks, then the cream. Add the spices, brandy and madeira. Mix all thoroughly and then test for seasoning by frying a small piece.

Grease a 2 lb bread tin, roll out two-thirds of the pastry and line the tin with it. Put in a layer of the forcemeat, then a layer of the meat strips, and continue until both are used up, ending with a layer of forcemeat.

Roll out the remaining third of the pastry and use it to make the lid, sealing the edges well. Decorate as elaborately as possible, and make one or two vents for the steam to escape.

Bake at 400°F for half an hour, lowering the temperature then to 350°F for a further hour. Half an hour before the end of the cooking time, take it out of the oven and glaze with beaten egg; return it to the oven and leave to finish cooking.

Take pâté out of the oven and allow to cool. Loosen the sides from the tin with a wet knife and turn it out carefully. Take off the pastry lid and pour in enough just-melted well-flavoured aspic to come over the top of the meat. Replace the lid and leave the pâté overnight. This should be eaten fairly quickly or the pastry will toughen.

David Collins' Pâté (for 6–8)

¾ lb lean pork
¾ lb pigs liver
½ lb belly pork, rind removed
2 large onions
2 eggs
2 oz butter
Coffee cup double cream
Wine glass white wine
½ sherry glass port
½ sherry glass brandy
1 fat clove garlic, crushed
1 pinch ground cloves

1 pinch ground mace
Salt and freshly ground pepper
Bay leaves and juniper berries
   for decoration.

Mince the meat finely. Put the port, brandy, garlic, cloves, mace, salt and pepper into a large bowl and add the minced meat to this. Mix thoroughly and leave for several hours.

Beat the eggs and stir them into the meat. Chop the onions finely and cook them in the butter, with a bay leaf, until soft and golden. Add the white wine and allow to bubble fiercely. Thicken with a little cornflour, and then add the cream to make a thick sauce. Remove the bay leaf and add this onion sauce to the meat. Fry a small sample to check for seasoning.

Put into the terrine, decorate the top (or bottom) with bay leaves and juniper berries, and cook for 1½ hours, covered, *au bain-marie* (standing in a baking-tin of water) at 350°F.

Pâté de Foies de Volailles (for 10–12)

1½ lb belly pork, rind removed
1½ lb cheap cut of veal
2 lb chicken livers
½ lb streaky unsmoked bacon
8 oz butter
1 tblsp salt
Bacon rashers to line terrine

1 dstspn *quatre-épices*
1 small onion
4 cloves garlic
6 juniper berries
8 peppercorns
½ pint white wine
¼ pint brandy

Mince the veal, pork, bacon and half the chicken livers finely. Chop the onion and garlic and mix into the forcemeat, together with the spices and alcohol; keep back some of the brandy and soak the rest of the chicken livers in it (having first trimmed them, but leaving them whole). Leave both forcemeat and livers overnight.

Next day, test the forcemeat for seasoning. Line one large or two small terrines with the bacon rashers, put a layer of forcemeat in, followed by the whole livers, and cover them with the rest of the forcemeat.

Bake at 350°F for 1½–2 hours (depending on whether you are using one or two terrines), covered, in a baking-tin of water. Remove the foil or lid for the last ¼ hour. Weight gently and store for a few days before eating.

Liver and Pork Pâté (for 6)

1 lb pigs' liver
½ lb belly pork, rind removed
1 oz pork fat
1 tblsp red wine
1 tblsp brandy
1 headed teasp salt
8 peppercorns

4 juniper berries
½ clove garlic

Mince the liver and pork finely and mix together. Crush the juniper berries, peppercorns, salt and garlic together and add to the forcemeat, together with the wine and brandy.

Mix very thoroughly and leave to stand. Fry a small piece to test for seasoning. Pack into a small terrine, and arrange the strips of pork fat on the top. Stand in a pan of water and cook at 330°F for 1 hour. Remove the cover and cook for a further 15 minutes.

Pâté de Foie Gras en Brioche

This recipe cheats by using a tin of *foie gras* – you have to make the brioche.

1 tin *pâté de foie gras* – the best you
   can find
6 oz plain flour
2 eggs
4 oz soft butter

½ teasp salt
½ oz fresh yeast or ¼ oz dried
   yeast
2 tblsps lukewarm water
Pinch of sugar

Dissolve the yeast in the water, adding a pinch of sugar; leave in a warm place until frothy. Meanwhile, sift the flour with the salt into a bowl and make a well in the middle of it. Break in the eggs and add the yeast mixture. With a wooden spoon, bring the flour into the eggs and yeast and beat until smooth. Add the soft butter in small pieces, beating hard. It will be hard work as the dough should be fairly stiff. Knead the dough with your hands, adding sprinkles of flour if it is too sticky to work, until it is smooth and elastic. Flour a plate, put the ball of dough on it and cover with a clean cloth, leaving it until double in size (about 1–2 hours in a warm kitchen). Knead again and leave in a cool place until you are ready to use it.

Remove the pâté from its tin and pour 2 tblsps brandy over it. Leave it to wait for the dough.

About an hour before eating, preheat the oven to 400°F. Flatten out the dough with your hands and wrap the *foie gras* in it, damping the edges and pinching them together underneath. Fit this into a greased bread tin, criss-crossing the top with a knife and brushing it with beaten egg or top-of-the-milk. Leave it to prove again for a further 15 minutes before putting it in the centre of the oven and baking for 30 minutes. Serve hot, with a glass of very good claret.

Pâté de Foie (for 4–6)

1 lb pigs' liver
6 oz unsmoked bacon
6 oz mushrooms
1 small onion
Salt and freshly ground pepper
1 clove garlic

1 oz butter
2 tblsps sherry
Thyme and parsley
Shortcrust pastry
   (optional, see recipe)

Cut the liver and bacon into large pieces and cook them in the butter long enough to stiffen them. Put this to one side and cook the finely chopped mushrooms, onion, garlic and parsley in the same pan, adding more butter if necessary.

Mince the liver and bacon and mix thoroughly with the mushroom mixture. Strip the leaves from the stalk of thyme and add, with the salt, pepper and sherry. Taste for seasoning.

Pack into a small terrine and cover either with a lid of shortcrust pastry (in which case you can eat it hot), or foil and a lid if you prefer it cold. Put it in a baking-tin of water and cook at 350°F for about 1 hour.

Basic Game Pâté (for 6)

1 pheasant
2 lb belly pork, rind removed
½ lb pork fat
2 eggs
5 fl oz brandy and dry sherry,
    mixed
2 teasps *quatre-épices*
3 teasps salt
5 crushed juniper berries

Freshly ground pepper
Bacon rashers

Part-roast the game for 20 minutes in a moderate oven. Leave to cool, then remove the flesh. Reserve the neat pieces of meat, and mince the scrappy bits finely with the pork.

Beat the eggs well and add them to the meat, together with the seasonings and sherry and brandy. Leave for the flavours to blend, then taste for seasoning in the usual way. Cut the pork fat into thin strips.

Line the terrine with bacon rashers, and layer the forcemeat with the pieces of game mixed with the pork fat strips; finish with a layer of forcemeat. Decorate with juniper berries and bay leaves, or cranberries, and lay the strips of rind from the belly pork in a lattice design over the top, to baste the pâté as it cooks. Cook, at 350°F in a baking-tin half-full of water, for 1¼ hours. Weight gently and store for a week in the winter.

Any game birds can be treated in the same way, two being used if they are small.

Duck Pâté with Green Peppercorns (or 8–10)

1 large duck
¾ lb belly pork, rind removed
½ lb cheap veal
½ lb pork fat
2 large chopped onions
1 oz butter
5 fl oz port
3 tblsps brandy
2 teasps *sel-épicé*

3 crushed allspice berries
2 tblsps green peppercorns
1 clove garlic

Bone the duck, following the instructions on page 85 if you have never done this before. Mince the pork and veal through the medium screen, take half of this and put it through the fine screen.

Cut the pork fat into cubes and mix with the minced meats. Cook the finely chopped onion and garlic in the butter until golden, and add the port. Bring to the boil and let it bubble vigorously for a minute or two. Allow to cool a little before adding to the meat; add the spices as well, and the green peppercorns, crushing them with the blade of a knife. Taste for seasoning in the usual way and leave to stand for an hour or two.

Lay the duck out flat and season it with more *sel-épicé*, sprinkle it with the brandy and spread it with the forcemeat. Fold the skin round it and sew it up down the back with strong thread – it will automatically re-form into something approaching a duck shape.

Put the duck in a roasting tin in a hot oven long enough to brown it, then lower the temperature to 325°F for another 1¼ hours. Drain off the fat from time to time, if there is a lot.

Do not weight this pâté as it will spoil the shape. This is a very good one to make for Christmas (remember to remove the thread before serving).

Pâté de Canard en Croute (for 8–10)

Omitting the green peppercorns, and using *quatre-épices* instead of *sel-épicé*, bone a duck and stuff it with forcemeat as in the preceding recipe. Sew it up firmly, and then tie it into a sausage-shape with tape.

Brown this duck sausage in clarified butter in a large frying pan. When well-browned, remove it from the pan and allow to cool. When cool, remove the tapes but not the thread. Meanwhile, make the pastry:

1½ lb plain flour
3 oz lard
4 oz butter
2 lightly beaten eggs

½ teasp salt
1 teasp icing sugar
¼ pint cold water (approx.)

Sift the flour with the salt and icing sugar and rub in the fats. Make a well in the middle, and pour in the beaten eggs. Mix these in, adding water when necessary, until you have a ball of firm paste. Put it in the refrigerator while the duck cools.

While the duck is still warm, roll out two-thirds of the pastry into a rough oval. Place the duck in the middle, breast up. Roll out the remaining pastry and fit it over the duck's breast. Damping the edges of the pastry, pinch together the top and bottom sheets until you have a neat parcel.

Decorate as you like with pastry trimmings and brush with beaten egg. Place on a baking-sheet in the centre of the oven heated to 425°F. Lower the heat to 350°F after about 20 minutes. Bake at this temperature for another 1¾ hours, placing it lower in the oven if it is getting too brown. Allow to cool for 24 hours, but do not put in the fridge as this spoils the pastry.

Pheasant and Pork Pâté (for 6–8)

1½ lb belly pork, rind removed
½ lb pork fat
6–8 rashers unsmoked bacon
1 large pheasant
2 teasps *sel-épicé*
2 tblsps each brandy and white
  wine

2 oz pistachio nuts
Handful of celery leaves and
  parsley
Scrap of garlic
Freshly ground pepper

Part-roast the pheasant as in the recipe for Basic Game Pâté. Remove the flesh as neatly as possible (use the scrappy bits for a pie and the meaty carcase for soup).

Mince the pork and half the fat finely; cut the other half of the fat into small cubes. Blanch the pistachio nuts and chop them roughly; chop the garlic, celery and parsley finely. Add the nuts, herbs, garlic, *sel-épicé*, pepper and alcohol to the pork and cubed fat, and mix these together thoroughly. Season the pieces of pheasant and sprinkle a little extra brandy over them. Leave them and the forcemeat overnight in a cool place.

Next dry, fry a small piece of the forcemeat to test for seasoning. Line a terrine with half the rashers, put in a layer of forcemeat and then a layer of pheasant pieces, continuing in this way until both are used up, finishing with a layer of forcemeat. Arrange the rest of the bacon over the top. Cook, in the usual way, at 350°F for about 2 hours. Weight it gently as it cools. Store for a week in the winter.

A Pâté de Foie de Porc from Périgord

1 lb fat belly pork	Bacon rashers
1 lb pigs' liver	Small glass brandy
3 shallots	1 carrot
Pinch nutmeg	1 onion
Pinch ground cloves	Freshly ground black pepper
1 teasp salt	Small glass white wine
1 pigs' trotter, split	1 bay leaf, sprig parsley, sprig
2 cloves garlic	thyme, strip orange peel

Mince the liver and pork finely, add the chopped garlic and shallots, the nutmeg and cloves, salt and pepper. Leave to stand then fry a piece to test for flavour.

Line the terrine with the bacon; pile in the liver mixture. Arrange the split pig's trotter, the sliced onion and carrot, the bay leaf, parsley, thyme and orange peel on top. Sprinkle with a little extra salt, pour the brandy and white wine over the top, and a little water to come level with the top of the meat.

Cover with foil, or a lid, and cook very slowly for 3–4 hours at 300°F. When it has cooled, but before the jelly has set, remove the trotter, herbs and vegetables. This is a good way of surrounding a pâté with aspic made as it cooks and it can be used with many terrines too.

Veal and Pork Pâté

Prepare 1 pint well-flavoured aspic according to the recipe on page

1 lb boneless veal	Chopped chervil and tarragon, or
1 lb fat pork	celery leaves and parsley
6 oz unsmoked bacon	A little thyme
2 cloves garlic	About 5 fl oz white wine
Nutmeg	2 teasps salt
	Freshly ground pepper

Mince the meat finely. Season with the finely chopped garlic and herbs, and the spices. Stir in the wine. Test for seasoning in the usual way.

Put the forcemeat into a terrine and pour in the melted aspic to come level with the top of the meat. Decorate the top of the pâté as liked and cover the terrine with foil, or its own lid. Cook, in a baking-tin of water, for 1¾ hours at 350°F.

When cold, pour over the rest of the aspic. This pâté can be stored for some time by pouring a layer of just-melted lard over the top of the aspic when it has set, to a depth of about ¼". Do not freeze.

Terrines

As I explained in my introduction, the name 'pâté' and 'terrine' are very often interchangeable in French charcuterie now. In my mind however, the difference lies in the fact that a terrine is generally a humbler, more everyday dish. It is something to have available in larder or fridge for lunch or supper, or packed lunches. The ingredients are simpler, the seasoning less subtle (but should be added just as carefully), and the texture coarser, than in the pâté. On the whole, these rustic French and modern English recipes are rather different from the traditional English 'tureens'; I have included a Northumbrian country version of a tureen, still prepared today and called a 'mitton', although no one can tell me why, and a recipe for a modern tureen of sweetbreads which is based on Victorian recipes for tureens and puptons.

Terrine de Campagne (for 6–8)

¾ lb cheap, lean veal
¾ lb belly pork
4 oz pigs' liver
4 oz pork fat
Small glass dry sherry

½ dstspn *sel-épicé*
6 crushed juniper berries

Chop half the pork fat into small cubes and reserve the rest. Mince the liver, veal and pork through the medium screen. Mix with the cubes of fat, the seasonings and sherry. Leave it to stand, then test for seasoning in the usual way.

Pile the mixture into a terrine and arrange bay leaves and the rest of the pork fat on top. Cover the dish and bake in a tin of water, at 350°F, for 1¼ hours, removing the lid for the last ¼ hour. Keep for a day or two before eating.

Devonshire Hare or Venison Tureen (for 8)

Legs and forelegs of a hare (reserve
the saddle for roasting), or 1½ lb
venison
¾ lb salted belly pork (page 83)
2 small onions
2 small bouquet garni of thyme,
marjoram, parsley, bayleaf and
strip of orange peel

Salt and freshly ground pepper
Large glass port
Bacon rashers
Flour and water paste

Choose a terrine with a well-fitting lid and line it with bacon rashers. Bone
the hare legs (the bones, and ribs, will make a lovely rich soup) and chop
(not mince) the flesh, and the pork. Chop the onions finely and stir them
into the meat mixture. Taking the saltiness of the pork into account, add salt
and pepper.

Pack the meat into the bacon-lined terrine and bury the bunches of
herbs in the middle. Pour the port over the contents.

Make a stiff paste from flour and water, roll a long strip between the
palms of your hands and fit it round the dampened rim of the terrine. Damp
the edges of the lid and fit this on top. If there is an air-hole in the lid, seal
this too with a blob of the paste.

Bake in a low oven (about 275°–300°F) for about 4 hours, or overnight. It
can be left for at least a week in the winter before breaking the seal of paste.

Duck and Pork Terrine (for 6–8)

1 small duck
1½ lb belly pork
½ lb salt pork (page 83)
8 juniper berries

3 tblsps madeira
2 teasps salt
1 clove garlic
10 peppercorns

Part-roast the duck for 15–20 minutes in a moderate oven. Remove the flesh
and reserve the neat pieces. Mince the scrappy bits with the belly pork
through the medium screen. Cut the salt pork into small dice. Mix the
crushed juniper berries, peppercorns and garlic with the madeira and add to
the meats, stirring thoroughly. Leave to stand.

Test for seasoning. Put a layer of the forcemeat into the terrine, then a
layer of duck pieces and cubes of salt pork; continue until all is used up,
finishing with a layer of forcemeat.

Cover with a lid, or foil, and cook for 1½ hours in a baking-tin of water, at 350°F, removing cover for the last 15 minutes. Weight the terrine while cooling.

Chicken Liver Tureen (for 4–6)

12 whole chicken livers
6 rashers unsmoked streaky bacon
2 finely chopped shallots
1 lb pork forcemeat (page 84)
Shortcrust pastry
  (optional, see recipe)

Salt, freshly ground pepper
Pinch mace
Pinch thyme
Small glass dry sherry

Having made the forcemeat, taste it for seasoning by frying a small piece. Use half of it to line a terrine.

Sauté the shallots in a little butter; season the chicken livers before tossing them in the butter for just long enough to seal the outside. The livers should be coated with the shallots already in the pan. Wrap each liver in half a rasher of bacon and pile these liver parcels on top of the forcemeat in the terrine. Pour the sherry over them, then put on the rest of the forcemeat in the terrine. If you want to eat the tureen hot, make a lid of pastry for the terrine; if not, then cover with the lid or foil as usual. Bake for 1½ hours in a moderate oven.

Terrine de Lapin (for 6–8)

A rabbit weighing about 1½ lbs
1 lb belly pork
¼ lb fat unsmoked bacon
Rind of ¼ lemon
Garlic

Pinch of nutmeg
Fresh thyme
6 crushed juniper berries
2 tblsps brandy
Bay leaf

Simmer the jointed rabbit in a little stock or cider for about ½ hour. Take the flesh off the bones and mince it coarsely with the pork.

Chop as much garlic as you like, a good sprinkling of fresh thyme, 6 juniper berries and a small piece of lemon peel, using a mezzaluna if you have one. Add this mixture to the meat. Season it highly with freshly-ground pepper, salt and nutmeg, and test by frying. Add the brandy.

Line a terrine with the bacon, add the forcemeat and cover with more bacon. Steam, covered, in a baking-tin of water at 325°F for 1½ hours. Weight it as it cools. A good light summer terrine.

Terrine de Lièvre (for 6–8)

About 2 lb hare	6 black peppercorns
1½ lb belly pork	Small glass red wine
½ lb pork fat	2 tblsps brandy
1 large teasp *sel-épicé*	6 juniper berries

Put the joints of hare to roast in a hot oven for about 20 minutes. Strip the flesh from the bones and mince it with the belly pork through a medium screen. Chop half the fat into cubes. Mix the meat, the alcohol and the crushed spices and leave for the flavours to blend before tasting a small piece.

Line the terrine with rashers of pork fat, if you can get them, or rashers of unsmoked bacon. Put in the meat mixture, decorate the top with bay leaves and cranberries or juniper berries, and lay more fat, or fat bacon, over all. Cook in the usual way at 350°F for about 1½ hours. Leave for at least 3 days before eating.

Italian Pork Cheese

'Chop, not very fine, one pound of lean pork with two pounds of the inside fat; strew over, and mix thoroughly with them three teaspoonsful of salt, nearly half as much pepper, a half-teaspoonful of mixed parsley, thyme, and sage (and sweet-basil, if it can be procured), all minced extremely small. Press the meat closely and evenly into a shallow tin – such as are used for Yorkshire puddings will answer well – and bake it in a very gentle oven from an hour to an hour and a half: it is served cold, in slices. Should the proportion of fat be considered too much, it can be diminished on a second trial. Minced mushrooms or truffles may be added with very good effect to all meat-cakes, or compositions of this kind.' From *Modern Cookery* by Eliza Acton, 1847

Terrine 'Petit Salé' (for 6–8)

¾ lb salt belly pork (page 83)
½ lb pigs' liver
1¼ lb belly pork, rind removed
2 tblsps brandy

10 peppercorns
10 juniper berries
1 teasp salt
2 cloves garlic

Mince the meat through the medium screen. Mix in the seasonings and brandy and leave to stand for 2 hours. Test for seasoning, especially salt.

Arrange some bay leaves in a pattern on the bottom of the terrine before piling in the mixture. Put the pork rinds on top of the meat, in a lattice pattern. Bake *au bain marie* for 1½ hours at 350°F, taking the lid off for the last 15 minutes.

Pigeon Terrine (for 6–8)

2–3 large pigeons
1 lb belly pork
6 unsmoked bacon rashers
Salt and freshly ground pepper

2 cloves garlic
6 juniper berries
2 tblsps port
Pinch of thyme

Braise or part-roast the pigeons for 10–15 minutes. Remove the flesh and mince it with the pork, and put half this combination through the fine screen again. Season with the salt, pepper, juniper berries and crushed garlic. Leave it to stand at room temperature for 1 hour, then test for seasoning.

Line a terrine with bacon, put in the forcemeat, pour the port over the top and cover with more bacon. Cover and steam in a moderate oven for 1½ hours. Remove the lid for the last 15 minutes. Weight it gently as it cools.

Northumbrian Mitton of Pork (for 4–6)

1½ lb sausage-meat from a reliable butcher
About ¾ lb unsmoked streaky bacon
Chopped mixed fresh herbs (be sparing with sage)
Salt and freshly ground pepper

Test the sausage-meat by frying a small piece and altering the seasoning, if necessary, to your own taste. Make small flat cakes of this sausage-meat and roll each one in the chopped herbs.

Line a greased pudding basin with bacon rashers and put in a layer of sausage-meat cakes, a layer of rashers, and so on until both are used up, seasoning lightly as you go. Fit foil directly on top of the meat and put a weight on top of that to keep the meat pressed down while it is cooking. Stand the basin in a baking-tin of water and cook for about 1 hour at 350°F, removing the weight and foil for the last 15 minutes. Drain off the surplus fat (but it will keep longer if you do not).

This can be eaten hot, and often is, but is also good cold (put a weight on it as it cools).

A Tureen of Sweetbreads

Make 1 lb veal and pork forcemeat (page 85)
1 lb sweetbreads
4 oz button mushrooms
1 truffle, if possible
1 oz flour

½ clove garlic
2 oz double cream
1 small onion
1 tblsp mixed fresh herbs
Strip lemon peel

Prepare the sweetbreads; soak them in warm, salted water for an hour or two. Drain them, put them in a small saucepan and cover with dry cider. Bring to the boil, lower the heat and simmer for 15–20 minutes. Pour off the liquid into a jug, and remove any hard bits from the sweetbreads.

Chop the onion and garlic and cook in the butter until golden. Stir in the flour, then gradually pour on ¼ pint of the liquid in which the sweetbreads were cooked. Cook this sauce gently for 10 minutes, until thick. Blanch the whole mushrooms for 2 minutes in boiling water with a squeeze of lemon juice. Drain them well and add to the sauce with the cream. Stir in the chopped herbs.

Line a deep terrine with two-thirds of the forcemeat. Pour in some of the sauce, then add the sweetbreads and chopped truffle, if used. Pour in the rest of the sauce. Cover with the remaining forcemeat. Put a lid of foil over the meat, then the lid of the terrine. Cook in a baking-tin of water in a low oven for 2 hours. This dish should be eaten hot, but is equally good cold. If you cannot get truffles, try asparagus tips, artichoke bottoms or even fresh peas.

Pork and Spinach Terrine

1 lb belly pork
1 lb raw spinach
About 4 oz sorrel, if available
2 oz pistachio nuts

1 teasp *quatre-épices*
2 teasps salt
Glass dry white wine
Freshly ground pepper

Wash the spinach and sorrel thoroughly, and cook them in the water that remains on the leaves, no more, over a low heat. When tender, tip them into a colander and leave them to drain, with a weight on top, while you mince the pork through the medium screen.

If the spinach still feels too wet, squeeze it dry with your hands. Chop it finely. Season the pork, add the white wine and the coarsely chopped pistachio nuts. Test for seasoning. Add the chopped sorrel/spinach mixture and mix thoroughly. A finely chopped clove of garlic can be added at this stage if you want. Cook, covered, in a baking-tin of water, for about 1 hour at 350°F, or until the meat has shrunk from the sides of the dish. Do not overcook. Another very good light summery terrine.

Galantines

Kettner, in his *Book of the Table*, ends his long entry on galantines with the depressing view that their preparation is best left to the professional – a negative attitude which I hope can be disproved by the recipes in this chapter. As you will see, dishes of this type originated on both sides of the Channel; the humbler brawn, also known as 'pork cheese', has an exact replica in the French 'Fromage de tête de Porc', and turkey galantine, beloved of the Victorians, in a *'Ballotine de Dinde'*. The preparations sound lengthy, indeed they are, but a small chicken, a pound of belly pork and a couple of pigs' trotters will make an elaborate and delicious dish to feed at least ten people. Do not be tempted to take a short cut by using packet or tinned aspic – the jelly is a by-product of the cooking process, and its clarification takes no longer than making up a packet. The flavour of a home-made meat jelly is incomparably better than that of any bought variety.

Basic Chicken Galantine (for 10–12)

1 3½ lb chicken	Large bouquet garni
2 pigs' trotters	Brandy
1½ lb belly pork	White wine
2 large onions, unpeeled	Salt
3 carrots, ditto	Freshly ground pepper
Fresh tarragon	1 teasp *quatre-épices*

Bone the chicken (see directions for this on page 85) and season it inside with salt and pepper, sprinkling it with brandy. Season the liver too. Leave it in a cool place while you prepare the forcemeat and stock.

Put the chicken carcase, giblets and split trotters, carrots, onion, bouquet garni, half-a-dozen black peppercorns and a large glass of dry white wine into a large saucepan. Add just a teaspoonful of salt. Cover with cold water and bring slowly to the boil; simmer for about 2 hours.

Make the forcemeat. Mince the belly pork, varying the texture to suit yourself, season with salt, pepper, white wine and brandy and test a piece in the usual way. Leave it to stand.

Strain the stock. Lay the chicken on a board, skin-side down, and spread it with a layer of the forcemeat. Put the liver in the middle – this will give a good dark centre to each slice when it is carved – and cover with the rest of the forcemeat. Sew up the chicken down the back with strong thread, tie it up firmly in a large square of muslin and lower into the gently simmering stock. Return the stock slowly to simmering point and keep at that heat for about 1 hour, longer for a larger bird. Remove it when cooked and allow it to drain on a china drainer. When the bird is cool, remove the muslin, and allow it to get quite cold.

Leave the stock to cool overnight, then remove all fat from the top. Reduce it, by fast boiling, by about one-third. Clarify it according to the instructions on page 84. Taste it and add a little sherry or white wine, and salt. Pour it into a shallow dish and leave to set.

Preheat the oven to 450°F. Remove the thread from the chicken and put it in the oven to brown, for about 20 minutes. Melt a little of the jelly and brush it over the breast of the re-cooled chicken; stick tarragon leaves in the jelly in a chevron design all down the front. When these have set, brush with a little more just-melted jelly. Serve surrounded with the rest of the aspic chopped roughly into cubes.

Brawn (for 8)

½ pigs' head, brains removed and reserved for another dish	Bouquet garni of bay leaves, thyme, parsley and celery leaves
2 pigs' trotters	Flavouring vegetables
6 peppercorns	½ pint dry cider

If possible, salt the head in brine for 24 hours – it will improve the flavour (see page 83 if you have no butcher who will do it for you). Have it chopped into manageable pieces when you buy it. Put the pieces into a large pan with the trotters, bouquet garni, peppercorns, vegetables and cider. Add 1 teaspoon salt, and cold water to cover. Bring to the boil, skimming frequently, then reduce the heat and simmer gently until the meat leaves the bones, which will take 2–3 hours.

Drain off the stock and reduce it. Season it with salt and anything else you feel is lacking. Pick the meat off the bones and season it with a little salt, black pepper and nutmeg. Add the seasoned meat to the stock in the pan and simmer both together for about 10 minutes. Taste it again when it is cool.

Before it sets, pour it into a pudding-basin rinsed out in cold water. Serve it decorated with plenty of fresh parsley.

Christmas Pheasant Galantine (for 6–8)

1 plump hen pheasant
1 lb fat, well-seasoned forcemeat
   (page 84)
4 oz finely minced chicken liver,
   plus the liver of the pheasant
4 oz truffled *pâté de foie gras*

3 shallots
2 rashers unsmoked streaky bacon
Crushed allspice and juniper berries
Brandy
Salt, freshly ground pepper

Bone the pheasant, sprinkle the inside with salt, pepper, allspice and juniper, and a little of the brandy. Mix the livers and chopped shallots with the forcemeat, test for seasoning, then spread over the inside of the pheasant. Lay the *pâté de foie gras* down the middle. Fold the skin over and sew it up down the back.

Ease the bird, breast up, into a terrine that just holds it. Arrange a pattern of cranberries and bayleaves (cut to look like holly leaves if you have time) on the breast, and cover with the bacon rashers. Put on the lid and cook in a baking-tin of water at 350°F for 1½ hours. Turn up the heat to 425°F and remove the lid for the last 20 minutes to brown the top.

Galantine de Canard (for 8–10)

1 large duck
1 teasp salt
½ teasp *quatre-épices*
1½ lb veal and pork forcemeat
(page 85)
2 pigs' trotters

2 tblsps brandy
5 fl oz port
2 carrots, unpeeled
2 onions, unpeeled
Bouquet garni
6 black peppercorns

Bone the duck and season the inside with salt, spices and some of the alcohol. Make a broth of the trotters, the duck carcase and giblets, carrots, onions, bouquet garni and peppercorns – no salt. Stuff the duck with the forcemeat and sew it up down the back; tie it up in a square of muslin. Simmer gently in the stock for 1½ hours. Remove and allow to cool before removing the cloth. Brown it in a hot oven. Strain the stock and reduce it by about one-third. Clarify it, taste and add salt and port. Allow it to set and use as for the Basic Chicken Galantine.

Ballotine de Dinde (Turkey Galantine) (for 12–14)

1 large turkey (about 14 lb)	3 eggs
1¾ lb lean pork	Salt, black pepper,
1¼ lb lean veal	*quatre-épices*
1 lb unsmoked streaky bacon	3–4 pigs' trotters
8 oz chicken livers	5 fl ozs brandy

Bone the turkey and remove 2 neat fillets from the breast. Salt and pepper the inside. Mince finely the veal, pork, bacon and livers and bind with the beaten eggs. Season with 3 teasps salt, freshly-ground black pepper and the *quatre-épices*. Test by frying a small piece. Spread half this forcemeat over the turkey, arrange the fillets in the middle and cover with the rest of the forcemeat. Sew up the bird and weigh it to calculate its cooking time (15 mins. to the pound). Tie it firmly in a muslin and try to get it into a neat sausage shape. Make a broth as usual from the bones, trotters etc. and cook the ballotine in this for the time you calculated (about 3½ hours for a 14 lb turkey). Leave it to cool in the broth. Unwrap the turkey and leave it overnight. Remove the fat from the broth, reheat it and strain it. Reduce it to 1½ pints and taste for seasoning. Pour it into a baking-tin to set. Brown the turkey in a very hot oven. Glaze it with some of the jelly and serve it surrounded by the rest.

Burgundian Ham and Parsley Galantine (for 8)
('Jambon persillé')

Large piece of gammon (about 4 lb)	1 peeled onion
½ bottle dry white wine or dry cider	2 cloves garlic
3 split pigs' trotters	2–3 oz finely chopped parsley
Bouquet garni of celery leaves, parsley, bay leaf.	
9 black peppercorns	

Put all ingredients, except the parsley, into a large saucepan, and cover with cold water. Bring to the boil, skimming off the scum as it rises, and then leave the contents to simmer until the gammon is well-cooked (about 2½ hours).

Remove the meat and flake it, putting it into a large bowl. Line a large sieve with damp muslin and strain the stock through it. Reduce it a little and taste for seasoning.

Add the parsley to the flaked ham in the bowl, mixing both well together. Pour the lukewarm stock over it and leave it to set (the ham should still be warm when you pour the stock over it). Turn it out onto a large dish and decorate with its own leftover jelly, roughly chopped, and sprigs of parsley. A very beautiful dish, eaten in the Burgundy region at Easter.

Galantine of Pork with Cider (for 8–10)

3 lb hand of pork, boned and
  rolled and the rind removed
2 pigs' trotters
¾ pint dry cider
2 washed, unpeeled onions
2 washed, unpeeled carrots

4 cloves garlic
Bouquet garni
Salt
6 peppercorns
6 juniper berries

The meat should be firmly tied into a neat sausage. Put it, the bones and skin removed from it, the trotters, seasonings and vegetables in a saucepan and cover with cold water and cider. Bring slowly to the boil, skimming the scum off from time to time. Let it all simmer very gently for 1½–2 hours. It should be very tender before you remove it from the pan. Leave it to cool.

Allow the broth to continue cooking for another ½ hour. Chop the meat roughly and pack it into a terrine or bowl which has been rinsed out with cold water. Keep the meat warm until the stock is ready. Strain the stock, taste it and pour a pint of it over the meat. Leave the rest of the stock to set and remove all the fat; reduce it by half, taste it and adjust the seasoning before clarifying it and allow it to re-set. Chop this jelly roughly and surround the pork with it; powder the galantine with chopped fresh chervil.

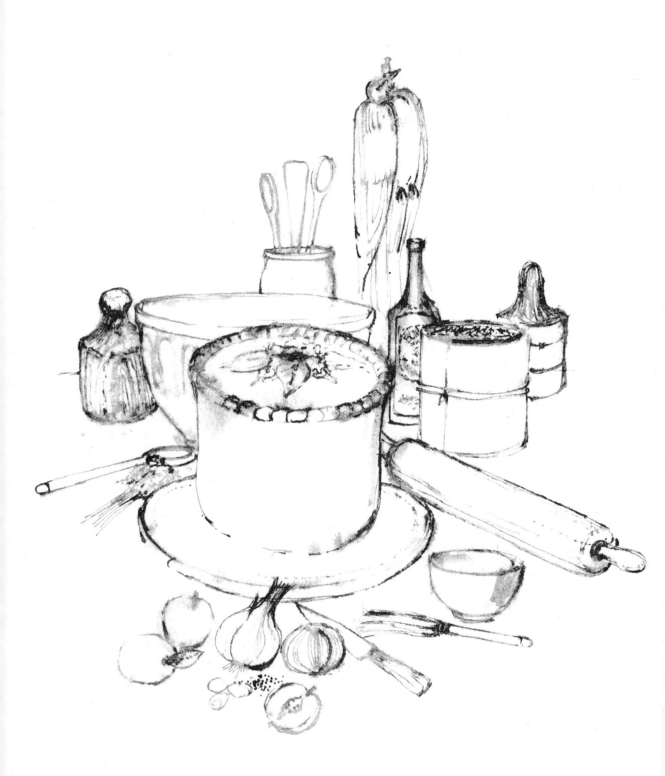

Raised Pies

The raised pie was one of the glories of the English table during the eighteenth and nineteenth centuries, and was matched in France by the pâté, originally baked in a pastry crust and therefore also qualifying as a pie. Brillat-Savarin, in *La Physiologie du goût*, published in 1825, mentions a 'pâté as tall as a church' offered to him as part of a breakfast by the monks of Saint-Sulpice. Milton, two centuries earlier, in *Paradise Regain'd*, has a similarly monumental turn of phrase to describe pies:

> 'A Table richly spred, in regal mode,
> With dishes pil'd, and meats of noblest sort
> And savour, Beasts of chase, or Fowl of game,
> In pastry built'.

The architectural quality of some of these great pies is easily imagined when even modern metal pie-moulds will turn out a pie as awe-inspiring as a Gothick tomb, and the texture of many commercial pork pies is often reminiscent of bricks and mortar. Raised pies were meant to be robust, they often had to travel to various parts of the country as presents from one member of a family to another, over appalling roads in badly-sprung carriages; but, as presents, they also had to taste good, and judging by old recipes they certainly did. I have included many old recipes in this chapter because there are few contemporary ones, but anyone who enjoys cooking can easily adapt them to suit her most available ingredients, and to any cook who says she finds pastry difficult, a hot-water crust is a godsend, being almost foolproof.

Hot-water Crust for Raised Pies

1 lb plain flour
7 fl oz water
6 oz lard
1 teasp salt
1 tblsp icing sugar

Put the water and lard into a small saucepan and bring to the boil. Meanwhile, sift the flour, salt and icing sugar into a bowl and make a well in the middle. When the lard and water have boiled and amalgamated, pour them, still boiling, into the middle of the flour. Stir the flour in until you have a ball of pastry in the bowl which leaves the sides clean. It will be too hot to handle at this stage, so cover the bowl with a teacloth and leave it to cool.

Prepare your mould: if it is a hinged metal one, all you have to do is grease it; if you are using a solid wooden one, or a glass jar, make sure these are well-floured, or you will find them very difficult to remove from the pastry.

When the pastry is ready to handle – still warm and malleable – roll out two-thirds of it and fit it into the metal mould, make sure you press it into all the mouldings, but being careful not to tear the pastry. Or, with the pastry flat on the table, put your floured Kilner jar or wooden mould in the middle, and fold the pastry up round it, pinching it and pleating it until it takes on the shape of the mould. If it slips down, it means the pastry is still too hot – leave it a little longer and try again. Leave the pastry to cool round the mould before gently easing them apart. You now have the container for whatever filling you are using.

Put the filling into the crust, piling the contents up into a gentle mound above the top of the pastry. Roll out the remaining one-third of paste, dampen the edges of the bottom and fit on this lid, pinching it with your fingers as you go. Make a neat round hole in the lid and put in a small roll of cardboard to keep it open while the pie cooks. When it is cooked, remove the cardboard and pour in just-melted meat jelly.

A pie raised up round a wooden mould may look less elegant than one made in a metal pie mould, but its homely appearance is no less appetising. The icing sugar gives a definite richness to the pastry.

Raised Pork Pie (for 4–6)

2 lb shoulder pork
½ lb piece lean bacon
Chopped fresh herbs in season
Salt, pepper, crushed coriander

About 1 pint aspic (page 82)
2 teasps anchovy essence

Mince the pork and bacon through the medium screen, or chop it by hand for a less dense texture. Mix in the seasonings. Fry a small piece, to taste, then pack the meat into the prepared crust. Put on the lid, make the air-vent, and decorate as elaborately as you like with scraps of pastry. Brush the pie with beaten egg and put it on a baking sheet in the centre of an oven preheated to 375°F.

Bake for 1½–2 hours, moving the pie lower in the oven and protecting the top with a piece of greaseproof paper if it is getting too brown. Allow the pie to cool for another hour or two, before removing the tube of cardboard and pouring in the just-melted aspic. Some recipes will tell you to pour in the aspic while the pie is still hot, but I have had best results with a lukewarm pie and jelly only just liquid enough to be poured.

Cheshire Pork Pie (for 4–6)

2 lb shoulder pork
3 medium Cox's apples
4 oz chopped onion
5 fl oz dry cider
1 tblsp brown sugar
Salt

Freshly ground pepper
   and nutmeg

Mince the pork coarsely, or chop it by hand, and chop the onion finely. Mix the two together and add the seasonings. Test a piece by frying it. Peel, core and slice the apples. Put a layer of pork and onion in the pie crust, then a layer of apple, and so on until both are used up, finishing with a layer of pork. Pour the cider over the top and put on the lid. Decorate as before, brush with beaten egg and bake at 350°–375°F for 1¼ hours.

The apple provides the moisture for this pie, which is as good hot as cold, so you do not need to add aspic.

Game Pie (for 4–6)

1 lb fat pork
½ lb thin-sliced streaky bacon rashers
1 lb game – pheasant, hare, venison, or a mixture
Small glass sherry or madeira
1 pint meat jelly made from the game bones as the recipe on page 82
Heaped tblsp chopped parsley and a little thyme
½ teasp *quatre-épices*
1 teasp salt

Mince or chop the pork and a little of the bacon; cut the game into neat pieces. Keeping the pork and game separate, season both with the salt, spices, herbs and alcohol and leave both to stand.

Line the pie crust with the rest of the bacon rashers, put in a layer of pork, then a layer of game and continue until the crust is full. Put on the lid and decorate, brushing with beaten egg.

Bake at 375°F for ½ hour, then lower the heat to 325°F for another hour. Leave to cool before pouring in the barely melted aspic.

Redcurrant, rowan or cranberry jelly are all very good with this pie.

Pigeon Pie (for 4–6)

3 pigeons
½ lb belly pork
5 fl oz red wine
2 tblsps red wine vinegar
2 chopped onions
Nutmeg
Aspic (page 82)
1 teasp fresh thyme
Salt, freshly ground pepper
Small glass port

Cut up the pigeons into manageable pieces, boning them if you prefer. Heat the wine, vinegar, onions, herbs and spices together in a saucepan and pour over the pigeons – leave in this marinade for 12–24 hours.

Chop the belly pork, drain the pieces of pigeon of their marinade. Season with a little more salt, freshly ground pepper and nutmeg and pack the pork and pigeons into the pie, finishing with a layer of chopped pork to baste the pigeons as the pie cooks. Pour in the glass of port and put on the lid. Decorate, make a hole in the top, and brush with beaten egg.

Bake for ½ hour at 375°F, lower heat to 325° and cook for a further hour. Pour in the jelly when the pie is cool.

Battalia Pie was popular in England in the seventeenth and eighteenth centuries, and was based on a French recipe called *Béatailles*: '*Béatailles* are all kinds of ingredients, that may be fancied, for to put together into a pye, or otherwise, viz. Cock's combes, stones, or kidnies, sweetbreads of veal, mushrums, bottoms of hartichocks etc.' From *The French Cook*, English version, published in London in 1654. I have taken the following recipe for Battalia Pie from Richard Bradley's *The Country Housewife*, published in 1753; it is obviously more curious than practical, but a combination of at least some of the ingredients, in smaller quantities, is very good. The 'Lear' with which he closes the pie is elsewhere given as consisting of 'Gravy, Butter and Lemons', and is probably a corruption of the French term *jus lié* – gravy thickened with butter and flour. 'Savoury balls' are forcemeat balls.

A Batalia Pye

Take four small Chickens and Squab Pigeons, four sucking Rabbets, cut them in Pieces, and season them with savory Spice; lay them in the Pye, with four Sweetbreads sliced, as many Sheeps Tongues and shivered Palates, two Pair of Lamb-stones, twenty or thirty Cocks-combs, with savour Balls and Oysters; lay on Butter, and close the Pye with a Lear.'

'Pulpatoons' contained ingredients similar to those found in Battalia pies, but the pastry crust was lined with a forcemeat before the poultry and sauce was put in. They are worth experimenting with.

'To make a Pulpatoon of Pigeons

Take mushrooms, palats, oysters, sweetbreads, and fry them in butter; then put all these into a strong gravy; give them a heat over the fire, then thicken up with an egg and a bit of butter; then half roast six or eight pigeons and lay them in a crust of forc'd meat, as follows: Scrape 1 lb of veal and 2 lb of marrow, and beat it together in a stone mortar, after it is shred very fine; then season it with salt, pepper, spice, and put in hard eggs, anchovies and oysters; beat all together, and make the lid and sides of your pye of it; first, lay a thin crust into your pattipan, then put in your forc'd meat, then lay and exceeding thin crust over them, then put in your pigeons and other ingredients, with a little butter on the top; bake it two hours.' From *The Compleat Housewife*, E. Smith 1742

I have included this next, very old, recipe for a steak pie because although it reads oddly at first, on a second reading you will see that it is very simple and calls for much less complicated ingredients than a pulpatoon. It is eaten hot, and the juice of a *Seville* orange (these do freeze well) squeezed over it before serving is delicious. A shortcrust pastry can be used instead of a hot-water crust.

'A Steake Pye, with a French Pudding in the Pye

Season your Steaks with Pepper and Nutmegs, and let it stand an hour in a Try then take a piece of the leanest of a Legg of Mutton and mince it small with Suet and a few sweet herbs, tops of young Time, a branch of Penny-royal, two or three of red Sage, grated bread, yolks of Eggs, sweet Cream, Raisins of the Sun; work altogether like a Pudding, with your hand stiff, and roul them round like Bals, and put them into the Steaks in a deep Coffin, with a piece of sweet Butter; sprinkle a little Verjuyce on it, bake it, then cut it up and roul Sage leaves and fry them, and stick them upright in the wals, and serve your Pye without a Cover with the juyce of an Orange or Lemon.' From *The Compleat Cook*, London, 1658. 'Verjuyce' was the juice of unripe grapes, for which you can substitute red or white wine.

Another recipe from Richard Bradley's charming book *The Country Housewife*, gives good and concise directions for making a Swan Pie. As swans rarely come the way of the ordinary housewife, it may seem a rather pointless recipe to quote here. However, the instructions cannot be bettered when making a duck or chicken pie. Make your hot-water crust in the usual way, lay the bird on the pastry and raise the crust round it with your hands, filling any spare corners with chopped and seasoned pork.

'A Swan-Pye

Skin and bone the Swan, lard it with Bacon, and season it with savoury Spice, and a few Bay-leaves powdered; lay on Butter, and close the Pye.'

Not all raised pies were made with meat and poultry, and this recipe of Mrs Raffald's for Salmon Pie can be adapted for other fish.

'A Salmon-Pie

Boil your salmon as for eating, take off the skin, and all the bones out, and pound the meat in a mortar very fine, with mace, nutmeg, pepper, and salt, to your taste, raise the pie, and put flowers of leaves on the walls, put the salmon in, and lid it, bake it an hour and a half, when it comes out of the oven take off the lid, and put in four ounces of rich melted butter, and cut a lemon in slices, and lay over it, stick in two or three leaves of fennel, and send it to table without a lid.' From *The Experienced English Housekeeper* by Elizabeth Raffald, 1794.

Yorkshire pies, as I have mentioned in my introduction, were famous for their size and solidity – Mrs Raffald's recipe demonstrates this and although it is one which is often quoted, I make no apologies for quoting it again, in full – it makes lovely and stimulating reading.

'A Yorkshire Goose-Pie

Take a large fat goose, split it down the back, and take all the bones out, bone a turkey and two ducks the same way, season them very well with pepper and salt, with six woodcocks, lay the goose down on a clean dish, with the skin-side down, and lay the turkey into the goose with the skin down, have ready a large hare cleaned well, cut in pieces and stewed in the oven, with a pound of butter, a quarter of an ounce of mace beat fine, the same of white pepper, and salt to your taste, till the meat will leave the bones, and scum the butter off the gravy, pick the meat clean off, and beat it in a marble-mortar, very fine, with the butter you take off, and lay it in the turkey; take twenty-four pounds of the finest flour, six pounds of butter, half a pound of fresh rendered suet, make the paste pretty thick, and raise the pie oval, roll out a lump of paste, and cut it in vine-leaves, or what form you please; rub the pie with the yolks of eggs, and put your ornaments on the walls, then turn the hare, turkey, and goose, upside down, and lay them in your pie, with the ducks at each end, and the woodcocks on the sides, make your lid pretty thick and put it on; you may lay flowers, or the shape of the fowls in paste, on the lid, and make a hole in the middle of your lid; the walls of your pie are to be one inch and a half higher than the lid, then rub it all over with the yolks of eggs, and bind it round with three-fold paper, and lay the same over the top; it will take four hours baking in a brown-bread oven; when it comes out, melt two pounds of butter in the gravy that comes from the hare, and pour it hot in the pie through a tun-dish, close it well up, and let be eight or ten days before you cut it; if you send it any distance, make up the hole in the middle with cold butter, to prevent the air from getting in.'

To come back to earth, here is a more prosaic recipe for a veal and ham pie to end the chapter. This was a great favourite on Edwardian picnics.

Veal and Ham Pie (for 4–6)

1 lb veal
1 lb ham, with a good
  proportion of fat
2 large eggs
Grated peel of ½ lemon
1 pint good aspic

1 finely chopped onion
1 tblsp fresh herbs
½ clove garlic
Salt and pepper

Hard-boil the eggs for 10 minutes – no longer or you will get those sinister grey rings round the yolks. Mince the veal and ham, and mix in the chopped onions, garlic, herbs, lemon peel, salt and pepper. Taste it by frying a small piece.

Put half the forcemeat into the crust and arrange the whole, shelled eggs along the centre, covering with the rest of the forcemeat. Put on the lid, make a hole in the centre and brush with beaten egg. Put the pie on a baking sheet in the middle of a hot oven – 425°F. Reduce the heat after 15 minutes and bake for a further hour at 350°F. Allow pie to cool for about 2 hours before pouring in the barely melted aspic.

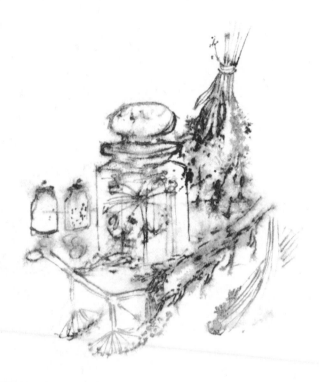

Potted Meats

As I have said in the introduction to this book, meat was 'potted' to preserve it, and to have a supply of cooked food always ready for any eventuality. Once the spice routes were open, and spices became cheaper and more available to all, not just the very rich, potting as a method of preservation was possible for most households. It is easily adapted to modern living; despite its usefulness for storing food for very long periods of time, the deep-freeze has one great drawback – the time needed for thawing the food. Try keeping a supply of potted meat or fish on hand and see for yourself how useful it is. Properly drained of liquids after cooking, well-spiced, and well-sealed with clarified fat, they will keep for months unopened – in a cold larder if you have one, or at the bottom of the fridge.

'To Pot Beef

Cut six Pounds of the Buttock of Beef into Pieces, season it with Mace, Pepper, Cloves and Ginger, beat together, and mixed with Salt; lay it in a Pot with two Pounds of Butter; bake it four Hours, well covered up; before it is cold take out the Beef, beat it fine, and put it down close in Pots, and pour on clarified Butter.' From *The Country Housewife* by Richard Bradley, 1753.

Castlegate Potted Pheasant

1 large old cock pheasant
5–6 oz butter (approx.)
Madeira
Clarified butter for sealing
  (page 83)

Salt, freshly ground pepper
Ground allspice
Lemon juice

The pheasant should be well-hung; if not, bring to the boil ¼ pint red wine, 2 tblsps red wine vinegar, a bouquet garni, and a small sliced onion and carrot. Let this get cold and pour it over the pheasant (plucked and drawn) then leave for 24 hours, turning occasionally.

Drain the pheasant and pat dry with a paper towel. Put it to braise, with a little butter, in a well-lidded pan, for about 45 minutes, or until well-cooked. Leave it to drain as it cools.

Remove all the flesh and weigh it. Calculate just over one-third of its weight and use this much butter. Mince the pheasant finely, beat in the soft butter, salt, pepper, allspice, madeira and a dash of lemon juice. Taste for seasoning as you go along.

Pack into scrupulously clean jars (washed out with soda and boiling water, if you have no dishwasher), filling them to within ½" of the top. Melt some clarified butter to cover the contents to a depth of ¼". Put the lids on the jars, or tie on foil or waxed paper caps. They can be stored safely for at least 2 months in the winter, either in a cold, dry larder, or at the bottom of the fridge. Once the seal is broken, eat within 2 days.

Char fishing in the Lake District has been revived as a tourist attraction, a pastime which in the eighteenth century gave rise to the popularity of potted char. This delicious and elusive fish, about the size and texture of a trout, with pink flesh like a salmon, is to be found in the deepest lakes. A permit is necessary if you want to try, but the permit is not difficult enough to procure to prevent the possible over-fishing which will result from the enormous numbers of tourists who visit the Lakes every summer. Char pots, shallow round dishes with a portrait of the fish on the side, can still be found in antique shops, but are collectors' pieces and usually expensive. If you are lucky enough to lay your hands on some char, potting it is perhaps the best way of eating it. I quote Elizabeth Raffald's recipe, and follow it with my version for potting trout, which are more easily available.

'To Pot Char

Cut off the fins and cheek-part of each side of the head of your char, rip them open, take out the guts and the blood from the back bone, dry them well with a cloth, lay them on a board, and throw on them a good deal of salt, let them stand all night, then scrape it gently off them, and wipe them exceedingly well with a cloth; pound mace, cloves, and nutmeg very fine, throw a little on the inside of them, and a good deal of salt and pepper on the outside, put them close down in a deep pot, with their bellies up, with plenty of clarified butter over them, set them in the oven, and let them stand for three hours; when they come out pour what butter you can off clear, lay a board over them, and turn them upside down, to let the gravy run from them, scrape the salt and pepper very carefully off, and season them exceeding well both inside and out with the above seasoning, lay them close in broad tin pots for that purpose, with the back up, then cover them well with clarified butter; keep them in a cold dry place.' From *The Experienced English Housekeeper* by Elizabeth Raffald 1794

Potted Trout

1 trout per person for a main course, or ½ each for an hors d'oeuvre
Salt, freshly ground pepper

Tarragon
8 oz clarified butter.

Ask the fishmonger to clean the trout and remove the heads and tails. When you get them home, put them on a board and press them firmly along their length with the palm of your hand – this loosens the backbone and makes it easier to remove. Slit the fish along the backbone, and lever apart with a sharp knife; the spine should leave the flesh easily, taking the other bones with it. You now have fillets of trout. Rub both sides of each fillet with salt and pepper and a little nutmeg, and leave overnight.

Next day, wipe each fillet with a cloth and salt-and-pepper each one again. Sandwich a sprig of fresh tarragon between each pair. Run about 1 oz clarified butter over the bottom of a terrine, and fit the fish in, head to tail and 'bellies up' as Mrs Raffald suggests. Cover them with more melted clarified butter, put a lid on the terrine and cook in a low oven (about 300°F) for 1½–2 hours. Test them with a skewer to see if they are done; drain off as much clear butter as you can, and throw away that which is mixed with the fish juices.

Put a china drainer over the terrine and turn the terrine upside down. The trout should end up safely on the drainer without breaking. Allow them to drain and cool. Remove the skin, together with any surplus spices, and the tarragon. Season them with a little more salt, pepper and nutmeg, and arrange in a very clean shallow dish. Pour over them the butter reserved from their cooking, plus any more necessary to cover them completely. Tie foil or waxed paper over the dish and store as before. They make a very good light summer lunch, with a cucumber and yoghourt salad and a glass of cold white wine.

Confits are the French version of our potted meats; they are very useful for adding to substantial winter stews.

Basic 'Confit' Recipe

2 lb boned shoulder pork, in ½ lb pieces
Jointed poultry – goose, turkey, duck
   or chicken
Jointed game – pheasant, hare, venison

   any, or all
   of these

For every 2 lb meat, mix: 1½ oz salt; ¼ oz saltpetre (from chemists); 2 crushed juniper berries; 4 crushed black peppercorns; pinch thyme and a crumbled bay leaf.

Rub the meat with the spice mixture and leave it overnight.

Sterilize the containers – wide-mouthed stoneware jars, or Kilner jars – with soda and boiling water, or by putting them in the dishwasher. Cold-water sterilising methods leave a faint but nasty taste. Cover the jars with a clean cloth until they are needed.

Take half the total weight of meat in best lard and melt it in a heavy saucepan; when it is hot, put in the pieces of meat. Put on the lid, which should be well-fitting, and cook gently, either in a low oven or on top of the store. Test the meat after one hour with a skewer; if it is tender remove it from the fat and leave it to drain – the saltpetre will have given the meat a pinkish tinge, do not be tempted to overcook because of this – if the meat is tender, it is done. Pour off the clear fat and reserve; throw away the rest.

Pour about 1½" fat into each jar and leave it to harden. Put in the pieces of meat, keeping the different sorts separate. Pour in more lard, to cover the meat and come level with the brim; it will shrink as it cools. Press a disc of waxed paper right down on to the surface of the lard, before putting on the lid of the jar, or a lid of foil.

Thus sealed, the confits can be stored for up to a year. To remove a piece of meat, stand the jar in a low oven until the lard melts and the meat floats to the surface. Remove as much as you need, and re-cool the jar, so that the fat closes over the remaining meat, topping up with more lard if necessary. Clear labelling, with the date, is important.

Either reheat the preserved meat and serve with mashed potatoes and some sort of sharp sauce (apple for the pork and goose, for instance), or add the pieces to stews made with fresh meat; especially useful when you have to 'stretch' a dish to accommodate an extra person.

Potted Hare, 1780

'Take 3 lb flesh of hare to 1 lb of pork or bacon fat and beat them together in a mortar till you cannot distinguish each from other. Season with pepper, salt and a large nutmeg, a handful of sweet herbs (sweet marjoram, thyme, parsley, all shred fine, double quantity of parsley). Beat all together till very well mingled, then put into a pot, laying it lower at the middle than the sides, and paste it up. Two hours will bake it. When it comes out of the oven, have clarified butter ready, remove the crust, and fill the pot an inch above the meat, while it is hot. When 'tis cold, paper it up, so keep it; which you may do three or four months, before 'tis cut. The fat of pork is much better than the fat of bacon.'

Lowestoft Potted Herrings

12 herrings, scaled, gutted, heads and tails removed
Freshly ground black pepper
Crushed allspice
1 crumbled bay leaf
Salt
Cider vinegar, or malt vinegar if you want to keep them longer

Make sure the herrings are dry before arranging them in layers in a deep stoneware casserole. Sprinkle each layer with the salt, spices and herbs. Press them well down before pouring on enough vinegar to cover them by about ½". Put a lid on the pot and put it into a low oven (200°F) and leave overnight. Take out next morning and store in a cool place. The fish will keep thus for about a fortnight in the winter, 1 week to 10 days in the summer. If you want to keep them longer, pour a little oil onto the surface of the vinegar. Very good as part of a mixed hors d'oeuvres.

If you have a good supply of pigeons available, try this recipe of Richard Bradley's. A cold potted pigeon for each person is delicious picnic food.

'To Pot Pigeons

Season your Pigeons with savoury Spice, put them in a pot, cover them with Butter, and bake them; then take them out and drain them; when they are cold, cover them with clarified Butter. The same way you may pot Wildfowl and Fish, only bone them when they are baked.,

Rillettes are another variety of French potted meat, particularly cheap, and quickly made.

Rillettes de Porc

2 lb belly pork
2 cloves garlic
Ladleful of water
Thyme, bay leaf, rosemary

Salt and freshly
   ground pepper

Remove the rind from the pork and chop the meat roughly into small cubes. Put it into a fireproof gratin dish with the chopped garlic, herbs, salt and pepper. Pour the water over the meat. Put the dish, uncovered, into the bottom of a low oven and leave until the meat is very tender, giving the contents of the dish a stir every now and then. It can be left all day, or overnight if you like.

Drain the meat carefully, as always, then pull it to pieces, using two forks, or a Zyliss Auto-chop (see Equipment). Do *not* put it in the blender. Taste for seasoning then pack into sterilised jars and seal with melted lard.

If you prefer a crunchier texture, have the oven a little higher so that the cubes of pork crisp at the edges; obviously it will then need less cooking time. The rind from the pork can be cut into squares and cooked on a higher shelf at the same time. Drain the squares of their melted fat, sprinkle them with salt, and you have *rillons*, or 'scratchings' as they are called in the Black Country.

Potted Shrimps

1 lb peeled shrimps
Powdered mace
Freshly ground pepper
4 oz butter

Cayenne pepper
Pinch of salt

Melt the butter slowly, then put in the shrimps and spices. Let them get thoroughly hot, without letting them boil, as this toughens them. Stir them as they heat. Put them into small pots and chill. Seal with a good ½" clarified butter.

Potted Tongue and Chicken

1 large chicken
Tongue weighing about 2 lb
2–2½ lb butter

3 teasps *quatre-épices*
1 dstspn salt

Bone the chicken (page 85). Boil and skin the tongue, trimming away the gristle and small bones. Mix the spices with the salt and rub the inside of the chicken with about two-thirds of this mixture. Place the tongue on top of the chicken and fold the skin up and round. Put this parcel, breast up, into a deep oval casserole. Scatter the rest of the salt and spice mixture over the top. Melt the butter gently and pour it over the chicken, covering it entirely. Seal the lid on with a flour and water paste (see the recipe for Devonshire Hare Tureen on page 42).

Put the chicken into a hot (425°F) oven for about 25 minutes, then lower the heat to 350°F for another hour. In the winter, you can put the entire casserole and its contents straight into the larder and keep it for at least a week without breaking the paste seal. When you want to eat it, remove the chicken, drain it and scrape off the butter, and decorate it with generous bunches of parsley or watercress. This is a good Christmas dish.

In the summer, remove the chicken as soon as it is cooked and leave it to drain. Leave the juices and butter in the casserole to get cold, then lift off the butter to use again. Replace the chicken in the clean casserole, melt the reserved butter and pour it over the chicken. Melt more clarified butter if necessary to cover it completely, and store in the bottom of the fridge until needed. Serve it in slices from the pot.

Potted Venison

2 lb boned venison
1 lb fat unsmoked bacon in a piece
2 cloves garlic
6 crushed juniper berries
2 bay leaves
1 dstspn crushed coriander
1 teasp crushed peppercorns

2 teasps salt
Red wine to cover the meat
Clarified butter

Cut the venison and the bacon into cubes, add the spices, bay leaves, and crushed garlic. Mix all well together and put into a terrine. Cover the meat with the wine, and the terrine with a lid and leave to cook as slowly as possible until the meat is tender.

Lift out the meat and let it drain until cold. Mince it finely, adding a little butter– no liquid– if the mixture is too dry. Check the seasoning, adding more salt and spices if necessary. Pot and seal with clarified butter.

Pastes and Butters

Commercial fish and meat pastes have, deservedly, a poor reputation and became branded, in the years between the two World Wars, as food of the poor. This reputation, coupled with the mistaken idea that *pâté* can be translated as 'paste', has given rise to the euphemistic use of the word pâté for what are in reality pastes – small amounts of cooked meat and fish, or cheese, pounded to a smooth consistency with butter. A totally different method to that used in the making of a real pâté, with its careful blending of raw meat, alcohol, herbs and spices, and long slow cooking, to produce a beautifully balanced and subtle dish.

Pastes evolved naturally from potted meats, and were served at breakfast and high tea. In 1946 the Wine and Food Society published a small book called *Pottery* by 'A Potter' (later revealed as Major Matthew Conolly, Cyril Conolly's father). Major Conolly remembers with relish the white china pots containing spiced tongue, or chicken, or anchovy, sealed with a crust of butter and often the work of one of the under-kitchen maids, which appeared on his grandmother's breakfast table. These pastes do still appear on our own tables, and in restaurants, offered as 'Kipper Pâté', or 'Chicken Liver Pâté' – very good they sometimes are, but they are *not* pâtés.

Pastes deserve a chapter to themselves in these days of expensive food: they are an excellent way of turning unattractive leftovers into delicious picnic food, or of glamourising a 'heel of cheese' into a dinner-party savoury. Venison or hare paste are both marvellous for a winter breakfast, and few people are ignorant of the delights of anchovy paste on toast for tea. I have also included one or two savoury butters, which make good hors d'oeuvres.

Anchovy Paste

4 oz butter
4 egg yolks
1 tblsp dry breadcrumbs

6 tblsps anchovy essence
Cayenne pepper to taste
Pinch of ground allspice

Cream the softened butter and beat in the egg yolks, one by one. Add the breadcrumbs and beat hard, then add the anchovy essence and spices. Place the basin over a saucepan of hot water and stir until the mixture thickens. Pour into small, clean jars and seal with ¼" clarified butter.

Chicken Liver Paste

8 oz prepared chicken livers
4 oz butter
2 tblsps madeira
Small piece garlic

1 dstspn crushed coriander
Salt and freshly ground
    pepper
Clarified butter

Chop the chicken livers roughly. Melt half the butter in a heavy frying pan and add the crushed coriander; let it heat for a minute or two before adding the chicken livers and garlic. Cook them over a medium heat to seal the outsides. Pour the contents of the pan into the blender and blend until smooth. Melt the rest of the butter and add the madeira, stirring all the time; bring to the boil and allow to bubble. Pour this into the blender and blend again. Add salt and pepper and taste, adding more coriander if you like. Pour into a jar and seal with clarified butter.

The coriander and madeira give this version a different and subtle flavour. Game livers can be treated in the same way.

Ham and Chicken Paste

6 oz cooked chicken
4 oz cooked ham
5 oz soft butter
Clarified butter

Salt
Freshly ground pepper
A little fresh thyme
1 bay leaf

Mince the ham and chicken finely and blend with the butter until thoroughly mixed. Season to taste with the salt, pepper and chopped fresh thyme, or tarragon in season. Put the bay leaf at the bottom of the pot and pile in the paste on top. Allow it to stand in the kitchen for an hour before sealing with clarified butter and storing in a cool dry place.

Herring Roe Paste

8 oz soft herring roe,
  cooked
Salt and freshly ground
  pepper

Few drops lemon juice
1 oz butter
2 teasps anchovy essence
Clarified butter

Put all the ingredients except the clarified butter into the liquidizer and blend. Taste to check seasoning, adding more anchovy essence if it is too bland. Pot and seal with clarified butter. Very good with hot toast for high tea.

Kipper Paste

3 Isle of Man or Loch Fyne kippers
  (the better the kippers the better
  the paste)
3 oz soft butter

Freshly ground pepper
Juice of half a lemon
A little salt

Cook the kippers by pouring boiling water over them and leaving, covered, for 10 minutes. Skin them and remove the large bones. Put them with the butter and lemon juice into the liquidizer and blend. Taste, and season accordingly – you probably will not need much salt. This is best eaten at once, but you can seal and store it as usual if you like.

Smoked haddock can be used in the same way but choose carefully, 'yellow fillet' is too salty and has little flavour.

Mushroom and Tomato Paste

1 lb cleaned and chopped
mushrooms
2 skinned and chopped tomatoes
2 rashers unsmoked streaky bacon
1 large egg

2 chopped shallots
1 clove chopped garlic
1 oz butter
Clarified butter

Fry the onion, bacon and garlic in the butter until soft. Allow them to brown a little. Add the tomatoes, then the mushrooms, stir well and let them cook gently for about 10 minutes. Tip the contents of the pan into the liquidizer and blend until smooth, then put the purée through a sieve to get rid of the tomato pips. Return the mixture to the saucepan and place over a low heat; add the well-beaten egg. Stir constantly until the mixture thickens (do this over hot water if you prefer). Taste for seasoning before pouring into sterilised jars and sealing with butter. This makes very good sandwiches.

Prawn Paste

8 oz peeled prawns
3 oz soft butter
Chopped fresh tarragon or chervil
Juice of ½ lemon

Cayenne pepper, salt
Clarified butter

Chop a few of the prawns roughly. Blend the rest with the butter and other ingredients. Stir in the chopped prawns. Taste for seasoning. Put into a pot and seal with clarified butter.

Smoked Cods' Roe Paste (Greek Taramasalata)

8 oz smoked cods' roe
1–2 cloves garlic
1 cold boiled potato, or a slice of white bread, soaked in water and squeezed dry

Juice of ½ lemon
Salt and freshly ground pepper
4 tblsps olive oil

Soak the roe overnight in water to make the skin easier to remove. Drain it well and mash it smooth. Mix in the bread or potato to lighten the texture, and add the crushed garlic. Beat hard. Add the lemon juice and olive oil, alternately and gradually. Taste for seasoning before you add any salt. Pile it into a shallow dish, decorating it with black olives, a sprig or two of parsley, and lemon quarters. Eat within a few hours.

Tuna and Chicken Paste

4 oz tuna, drained of
   its oil
4 oz cold chicken
2 oz anchovies, drained

Freshly ground pepper
3 oz soft butter
Lemon juice
Clarified butter

Blend tuna, chopped chicken, anchovies and butter. Stir in the lemon juice and add the pepper. Taste. Pot and seal as usual.

Tuna on its own, or sardines, make a good paste for children's sandwiches, using the above method. Much nicer than bought fish-paste.

Pastes made from small amounts of cheese left in the larder make unusual savouries, and can be spread on toast and put under the grill to be served hot. With a lump of cold clotted cream on top they make a welcome change to puddings.

Stilton Paste

6 oz ripe Stilton   2 oz soft butter
Pinch of nutmeg   1 tblsp madeira or port

Mash the butter and Stilton together, stir in the nutmeg and port or madeira, and taste to see if it needs salt. Pot, and seal with a lid of foil. It is not necessary to seal with butter unless you want to store it for a very long time.

Walnut and Cheddar Paste

8 oz good Cheddar   2 oz roughly chopped walnuts
  (or Double Gloucester)   Few drops Worcester sauce
3 oz butter   ½ teasp Dijon mustard

Grate the cheese, and blend with the other ingredients. Taste for seasoning, adding a little more Worcester sauce if necessary. Pot and seal with a thin layer of clarified butter, or with a lid of foil.

Cheshire and Onion Paste

8 oz good Cheshire cheese   1 small chopped onion
3 oz butter   Freshly ground pepper

Grate the cheese and blend with the butter and the onion. Season with pepper and a little salt. This does not keep, because of the raw onion, but makes a very good lunch with brown bread, pickled onions and beer.

The following savoury butters can be served with grilled fish or meat in the traditional way, but are also delicious as hors d'oeuvres, straight from the fridge with very hot, thin toast – Melba toast, if you can manage it. This is how I first tasted Magdalen butter, in Oxford, of course, but I have since had it with grilled salmon steaks.

Epicurean Butter

4 anchovy fillets
Small bunch of chives
1 teasp chopped fresh tarragon
1 teasp Dijon mustard
4 chopped gherkins

Yolks of 2 hardboiled eggs
3 oz butter
1 teasp crushed green
  peppercorns

Chop the anchovies, herbs and gherkins as fine as you can and blend with the butter. Mash the egg yolks and add, with the mustard and green peppercorns. Taste for seasoning and put into small butter pots (one for each person) if you have them; if not, into any small shallow pot. Chill in the fridge and eat within a few hours. This can also be served with cheese.

Magdalen Butter

1 tin anchovy fillets,
  drained
Small bunch watercress

An equal weight of
  soft butter
Freshly ground black pepper

Remove the stalks from the watercress and chop it finely (some recipes recommend blanching it first, but this spoils its fresh flavour). Chop the anchovies. Blend the butter, watercress and anchovies and taste for seasoning, adding pepper, and a little salt if necessary. Chill and pot as above.

Tomato Butter

1 lb skinned and chopped tomatoes
Fresh basil or tarragon
Salt
Pinch sugar

8 oz soft butter
Scrap of garlic
Freshly ground pepper

Cook the tomatoes and garlic in a little butter, simmering fast until most of the juice has evaporated. Leave them to cool. Put into the liquidizer with the butter, herbs, salt, pepper and sugar and blend. Chill in shallow pots, and serve with lamb chops, or grilled fish, or as a first course with hot toast.

APPENDIXES

Appendix A: General Recipes

Aspic or Meat Jelly – for use in raised pies, and pâtés, and galantines.

4 oz shin beef
Fresh game, poultry or beef bones
2 large onions, unpeeled and stuck
with cloves
6 lightly crushed peppercorns

2–3 pigs' trotters
2 large carrots, unpeeled
Large bunch herbs
1 teasp. salt

Put all into a large saucepan and cover with cold water. Bring to the boil and skim. Lower heat and simmer gently, with the lid off, for about 3–4 hours (this can be done in the oven). Raise the heat and boil rapidly until you have about 1–2 pints. Strain the stock carefully and leave to get cold.

Remove the fat. Reheat the stock and taste for seasoning, adding salt, a little pepper, and sherry, cider or white wine, depending on what it is to be used for. If you want a clearer jelly, clarify it according to the method on page 84.

The pigs' trotters can be served cold with a vinaigrette sauce as an hors d'oeuvre, or dipped in egg and breadcrumbs, grilled and served very hot with quarters of lemon. The shin beef can be minced, mixed with half its weight in butter and made into beef paste.

The onion and carrot skins give the aspic a good golden colour. Do not freeze.

Brine for salting pork

If you do not have a butcher who will put pork into brine for you, you can do it easily at home. All the recipes calling for unsmoked bacon will benefit from your using salt pork. A piece of salted belly pork cooked like gammon and served with cabbage and a piquant sauce makes a delicious cheap winter meal. Choose a large stoneware jar with a lid and sterilise it with boiling water and soda. When you take a piece of meat out of the brine, reboil the brine with another 4oz salt before re-using it.

3½ pints water
12 oz cooking salt (block salt, preferably)
6 oz brown sugar
1 bayleaf

10 crushed juniper berries, peppercorns, allspice berries
1 oz saltpetre (from chemists)
1 sprig dried thyme

Put the water, sugar, salt and saltpetre into a large saucepan and bring to the boil. Tie the herbs and spices in a piece of muslin and add them to the pan. Let all simmer for about 10 minutes. Remove from the heat and leave to get quite cold before pouring it over the meat. Make sure the meat stays below the surface of the brine by fitting a saucer or small plate on top to keep it under. A week is usually long enough to salt a 2lb piece of belly pork.

To clarify butter

As clarified butter is useful to have in the kitchen, for frying fish as well as for sealing purposes, prepare it in large amounts and store it in labelled margarine or yoghourt tubs in the fridge. It will keep indefinitely.

Melt 2lb slightly salted butter over a gentle heat. Remove it when it has completely melted and let it stand for 5–10 minutes. Wring out a piece of muslin or an old clean handkerchief in very hot water and line a small sieve with it. Put the sieve over the container in which you are going to store the butter and pour the melted butter slowly through it. The butter will drip through, leaving salt and other impurities behind on the muslin. It is now ready for use.

To clarify stock for galantines and raised pies.
Use two egg whites for every 4 pints of stock. Beat the egg whites lightly in a saucepan, and add the crushed shell of one of the eggs. Pour on the lukewarm stock, which you have previously strained of its fat, meat and vegetables. Heat slowly, beating occasionally with a wooden spoon, until the stock starts to simmer. There will now be a greyish crust on the surface. Turn off the heat and leave the saucepan for 10 minutes.

Line a colander with muslin wrung out in hot water and stand it over a deep bowl. Pour the stock through slowly, leaving it to drip through. Taste it for seasoning if you have not already done so, before pouring it into a shallow dish (so that it can be chopped for a galantine), or into a covered bowl to be kept in a cold place until needed. It will not keep long in the summer.

Veal and pork forcemeat – for pâtés, galantines and any recipe needing a richer and more sophisticated forcemeat than the one which follows.

¾ lb lean pork	2 large onions
¾ lb lean veal	2 eggs
½ lb pork fat	1 oz butter
3 fl oz madeira	1 teasp *quatre-épices*
1 dstspn salt	1 tblsp chopped herbs
½ clove garlic	

Chop the onions and garlic and cook them gently in the butter until soft. Add the madeira and allow it to bubble fiercely for 2–3 minutes. Remove from the heat and let it cool. Mince the veal, pork and pork fat finely and mix in the onion mixture.

Beat the eggs well and add to the meat, then the spices and herbs and salt. Leave it to stand for an hour or two. Test a small piece by drying it, and tasting it for seasoning before using.

This forcemeat makes a good lining for raised pies, and a good stuffing for the more elaborate galantines.

Simple pork forcemeat

1½ lb belly pork, rind removed
½ lb back pork fat
1 teasp. *quatre-épics*
2 tblsps brandy

2 teasps salt
1 clove garlic
Chopped fresh herbs in season
¼ pint white wine

Mince the meat and the fat through a medium screen. Add the salt, spices, wine, brandy and herbs. Let mixture stand for an hour or two. Fry a small piece to test for seasoning before using. This quantity is enough to stuff a large chicken or duck. If you want to make your own sausages, this recipe is a good one to use.

Appendix B: Boning Poultry

'First bone your bird' has a daunting sound, but when you have done it once, and have grasped the layout of a poultry skeleton, you will probably find it easier than boning a leg of lamb. You need a good firm wooden board and a small sharp knife. If the bird has been frozen, make sure it is thoroughly defrosted first. Do not be tempted to make a start unless it is; I did once and found that my fingers got so cold that I cut them several times without noticing.

Lay the bird, breast down, on the board and cut down along the backbone from top to bottom. Holding skin and flesh in your left hand, follow the carcase of the bird round the left side, with your knife, always keeping close to the bone and sliding the knife between bone and flesh. Providing your knife is really sharp this will be easy. What you must avoid is puncturing the skin.

At the bottom left-hand corner of the carcase you will find the ball-and-socket joint where the thigh joins the body. Putting the point of your knife in the joint, lever it apart so that the leg parts from the carcase. Then slide your knife up along the leg bone, and all round it until the bone comes free of the flesh, separating it at the second joint as at the first. Leave the drumstick intact, as it will help to reconstitute the shape of the bird. Cut round the right side of the carcase and detach the right leg in the same way. You will now have something that looks like a pair of jodhpurs, still attached to the carcase along the breastbone and by the wings.

Still keeping the bird breast down, locate the flat bone at the top left-hand side of the back of the carcase, which approximates to our shoulder blade. Slide the knife under it and lever it from the body. At this point, cut off the wing tips altogether which makes it easier to go on removing the other wing bones from the flesh. Now you have a 'sleeve' as well and you are coming to the tricky bit where the skin is perilously near the breastbone. This problem can be dealt with by cutting away the flexible ridge of the breastbone with the skin. Once you are free of the breastbone, continue to separate flesh and carcase, *carefully*, all down the front. Then you can carry on and finish boning the other wing and detaching the carcase entirely.

If you find that the bones still have a lot of meat attached to them, remove it and mince it with the forcemeat so that it is not wasted. This shapeless garment that was once a recognisable bird will miraculously regain its shape when it has been stuffed and sewn up down the back.

Appendix C: Alcohol

Alcohol plays a vital part in the seasoning of a number of recipes in this book. It is not the alcoholic content that is important, of course, as this evaporates in the cooking, but the flavour and mellowness that the taste of the right wine gives to the mixture. Amounts used are generally small, so all this is not as extravagant as it sounds, but do not be tempted to omit the alcohol in the recipe in the interests of economy.

Brandy – French grape brandy can be bought fairly cheaply in half or quarter bottles, but buy the best you can afford.

Sherry, madeira and port – the sherry should be dry; madeira and port can be cheaper than you would normally drink. Keep the bottles tightly corked. In certain recipes, these three 'fortified' wines can be substituted for each other, so it is not really necessary to have all three in the larder at the same time.

Red wine – a bottle of cheap plonk kept for cooking only is best, but the better the wine the finer the flavour. There is a lot of very bad medium-priced wine on the market at the moment which should be shunned at all costs. For a constant supply of cheap wine for cooking and drinking, make your own from one of the many wine kits now available. I have had best results from Boots 'Beaujolais' and 'Claret', at about £1 a gallon, and with a little patience, you end up with a far better product than an over-labelled bottle from the wine merchant down the road.

White wine – the above remarks apply here too. With certain exceptions, always buy a dry white for cooking, and this also goes if you are making your own – try Boots White Concentrated Grape Juice for a good multi-purpose medium dry white wine.

Cider – a really good dry cider can be substituted for white wine, and is good in its own right. Bulmers Special Dry Reserve is very good indeed and is becoming easier to find. More expensive than the ordinary, sweeter ciders, it is much better, and still only half the price of the cheapest dry white wine.

A new series of 'wine flavourings' is just being marketed. Having tried them, I think it would be better to omit wine altogether than to use them. You cannot drink them, either.

Index

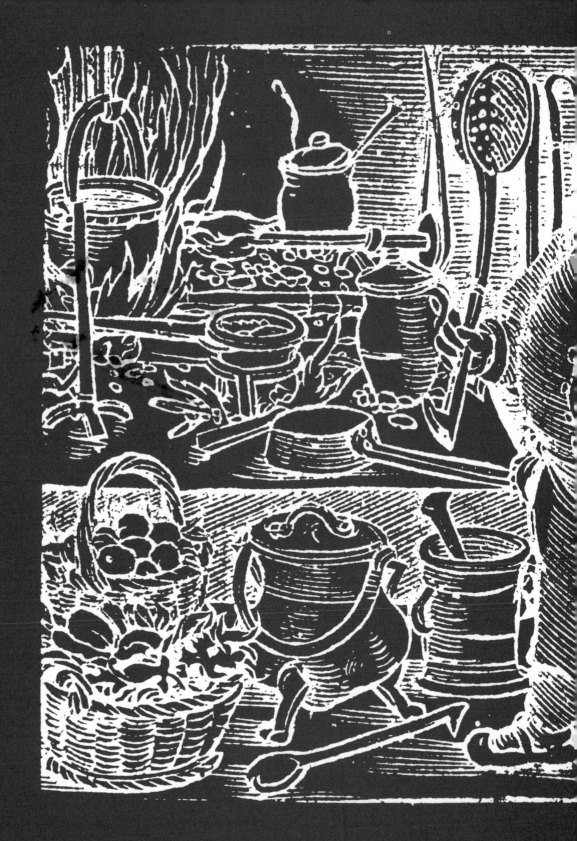